LONELY MYSTIC

A New Portrait of
Henri J. M. Nouwen

MICHAEL FORD

Paulist Press
New York / Mahwah, NJ

Cover image: Digital reproduction of the photograph of Henri Nouwen [detail] with Jutta Ayer (ca. 1986) from the Henri Nouwen collection of the Special Collections, Kelly Library at the University of St. Michael. Used with permission.
Cover design by Sharyn Banks
Book design by Lynn Else

Library of Congress Cataloging-in-Publication Data is available upon request.

ISBN 978-0-8091-5397-8 (paperback)
ISBN 978-1-58768-769-3 (e-book)

Published by Paulist Press
997 Macarthur Boulevard
Mahwah, New Jersey 07430

www.paulistpress.com

Printed and bound in the
United States of America

For Frank M. Hamilton

The true mystic is always both humble and compassionate, for she knows that she does not know.

—Richard Rohr

CONTENTS

ACKNOWLEDGMENTS

I am continually grateful to Henri Nouwen's family, friends, and colleagues for recording their memories of Henri a year after he died, and to those who have made special contributions to this study. My thanks to Frank Hamilton for agreeing to speak publicly for the first time about his friendship with Henri over many years; to Michael Harank for kindly allowing Henri's letters to him to be published in this book and for his perceptive comments on them; and to Chris Glaser for his astute reflections on his former teacher, along with new mystical insights.

    Many have supported my Nouwen work; among them are Joy Adams, David Birchall, Scott Brubaker, David Camilleri, Michael Christensen, Mary Garcia, Damian Hart, Peter Huxham, Willem Klaver, Kathy Loftus, Chris McDonnell, Sue Mosteller, Karen Pascal, Anthony Redmond, Lee Taylor, Raymond Tomkinson, and Mark Woodrow. Special thanks to Dr. David Torevell, who supervised my doctoral thesis on Henri Nouwen, for offering helpful feedback on the manuscript, and to my mother, Margaret, and brother, Nigel, for their encouragement. As always, I am grateful to my editor, Paul McMahon, for his caring and efficient guidance, and all the hard-working team at Paulist Press.

PROLOGUE

*The Christian of the future will be a mystic or will not
exist at all.*

—Karl Rahner, SJ

"The look in his eyes when they met your eyes revealed the
man's soul: his reassuring sympathy restored your confidence in
yourself. Just to speak to him made you feel better; you knew that
he was listening to you and that he understood you."[1]

  This evaluation of the great French mystic and priest, Pierre
Teilhard de Chardin, could easily pertain to the Dutch pastor,
Henri J. M. Nouwen. Most people I spoke to about him said something in that vein—and I saw it for myself. While Henri could be
restless and distracted, when he gave you his attention, he touched
your heart. One of the most compelling spiritual thinkers of the
twentieth century, Henri was wonderful with people. An outstanding teacher, public speaker, and writer, whose hugely popular
books have sold over seven million copies worldwide, the author
was a specialist travel writer in the sense that he recorded not only
the vicissitudes of his outer pilgrimage as a lonely pastor yearning
for intimacy, but also the struggles of his inner journey, trying to
come closer to God. Both experiences melded into one holy pilgrimage. Ordained a Roman Catholic priest at Utrecht Cathedral in

1957, Henri Nouwen then began his training to become a clinical psychologist, later leaving his native Holland for America to study religion and psychiatry at the Menninger Foundation in Topeka, Kansas—a time he described as being hugely influential. Professor Nouwen, as he soon became, held senior teaching posts at the University of Notre Dame, Indiana, and at Yale and Harvard Divinity Schools. Highly esteemed as a pastoral theologian and communicator, he became one of the most popular spiritual writers of all time with *The Wounded Healer*, *The Genesee Diary*, and *The Return of the Prodigal Son* among his most acclaimed titles. A long interest in the people of Latin America eventually took him to Peru as a missionary in his search for a vocation away from academia, but eventually he discovered his new calling in Canada—as pastor at Daybreak, a community for people with learning disabilities.

Gustavo Gutiérrez called him "an exceptional human being"—and so he was. Yet despite his phenomenal gifts, he was also an enigma and a paradox, a man tortured by deep personal anguish, uncertainty, and self-doubt. He shouldered a cumbersome insecurity, which took the form of a chronic need for admiration and a desperate fear of rejection. These deep-seated struggles, not unrelated to his uniqueness as a human being and the loneliness of his mission in life, culminated in a breakdown shortly after joining L'Arche in his mid-fifties, but he recovered to resume his priestly leadership and write more bestselling paperbacks. Always alert to new encounters with God, he befriended, in his final years, a flying trapeze troupe in Europe, where he discovered a novel theology of the body. Henri Nouwen died in Holland in 1996 and was buried with members of his community in Ontario.

Although I met Henri only once, we became friends and stayed in touch. It is fair to say there was a spiritual affinity between us, and for over a quarter of a century I have studied, taught, and given retreats and talks on Henri. A Benedictine monk even gave me a special blessing for my Nouwen mission. This took place on

Henri's birthday, which falls on the Feast of St. Francis de Sales, patron saint of writers and journalists.

I began my research into Henri's extraordinary life the year after he died. This appeared as *Wounded Prophet* in 1999.[2] In this new study, I attempt to show, through vivid testimonies unpublished until now, how the *contemplative* side of his character was not so much overshadowed by his emotional trials but rather driven by them. The man who turned down the chance to become a bishop and declined an invitation to have an audience with the pope was, in my eyes, one of the world's greatest spiritual luminaries and mystics, precisely because his immense psychological suffering resulted in remarkable insights about the soul and God.

At the time of my first book, I was a BBC radio producer and, in true reporting spirit, interviewed 125 people—far too many in retrospect, but by the time I had played back the last tape, I had formed a distinct impression about Henri. Clearly, Henri had been much loved by those who had known him, and all their recollections were consistent in describing his spiritual prowess and psychological make-up. Although the original interviews with his family and friends helped shape *Wounded Prophet*, it was, unfortunately, not possible to include all the information or anecdotes I had accrued. As any film editor knows, what ends up on the digital equivalent of the cutting room floor isn't necessarily unworthy or unsuitable. It's simply that there just isn't room, or other factors suddenly dictate that the allotted space must be curtailed. I stored the interview tapes for nearly two decades. Then one day, while preparing to give a retreat on Henri, I decided to dig out a few of the recordings as illustrative material. Hearing them again after such a long time was a moving experience, so I decided I would paint a new portrait from the remaining colors, the ones that hadn't been used before. In addition, Henri's spiritual confidant, Frank Hamilton, agreed to speak publicly for the first time about his close friendship with the writer. While several people have also provided me with additional, unpublished material to complete the picture, I have deliberately not undertaken any other interviews or drawn from any other accounts of his life, though I have extricated some relevant reflections from my doctoral thesis on Henri. Where some members of the original *Wounded Prophet* cast reappear, their quotes vary from what was incorporated from them at the time (except where it has been necessary, from the narrative viewpoint, to retrace a few steps). While the prominent landmarks of Henri's story are revisited to make sense of the journey, new voices contrast the profoundly spiritual Henri with the deeply human Henri to show that Christian mystics are neither inaccessible nor without their own foibles.

The rest of this prologue explores understandings of the mystical life and Henri's own thoughts. I retell Henri's life story from chapter 1, where I discuss his early days and priestly vocation, while Henri's psychological formation and early teaching career form the subject of chapter 2. Henri's contemplative development at the Abbey of the Genesee is discussed in chapter 3, which also shows how his spiritual growth there was the springboard for his missionary work in South America and his reverse mission to the United States. Chapter 4 includes further memories of his life at L'Arche and his care of Adam Arnett, who became a mystical presence in his life. Henri's belief that sexuality should be spoken about from a mystical, rather than a moral, perspective is the subject of chapter 5. Private letters sent to Henri's former secretary at Harvard around the time of his breakdown are revealed with commentary for the first time in chapter 6, while Henri's spiritual confidant, Frank Hamilton, speaks exclusively about the author in chapter 7. The public and private sides of the famous writer are featured in chapter 8, with his personal spirituality the focus of chapter 9. Henri's final years are analyzed in chapter 10, which includes an interview with the leader of the South African trapeze troupe he befriended. The epilogue assesses Henri Nouwen's place in the Christian mystical tradition with a contribution from the Franciscan speaker and writer Richard Rohr.

THE TOUCH OF GOD

One bright morning over breakfast in Minnesota, a quizzical professor watched intently as a colleague pulled out a handful of pills, among them a golden Vitamin E capsule. His eyes began to widen incredulously. Sunlight streaming through the window had suddenly struck the capsule at an angle, coating it with a mysterious aura. "Where did you get that?" he asked agog and in awe. "It's so beautiful." To his bemused assistant, it was a run-of-the-mill vitamin tablet, but to Henri J. M. Nouwen, natural-born mystic and world-renowned spiritual author, it had been transformed into a celestial gem as the interspersing light conjured an image of eternal beauty. Never short on childlike wonder, here was a middle-aged man enraptured by something many of us would take for granted, which was why, like a true contemplative, he tended to see what other people did not: that rare gift for detecting the extraordinary in the ordinary.

Henri was a mesmerizing Dutch Master, a popular artist of the spiritual, who was an even more intriguing person. He identified with the agony and the ecstasy of van Gogh, who signed his paintings "Vincent." While Nouwen's full name and initials appeared on his literary canvases, he preferred to be known simply as "Henri." From the drama of his professionally creative but, at times, tragically sad life emerged some of the finest religious books ever written. There was a secret to his success. He did not believe you should use a spiritual book as a source of information, but rather listen to it as a voice that addressed your heart directly. The text had to "read you." If you were hungry only for knowledge, it meant you wanted to own the word, rather than allowing the word to own you. Henri's spiritual writing flowed with this understanding in mind. Simplicity and emotional honesty could at times disguise the profundity of his words. His style was unadorned because, while he wrote in English, he thought in Dutch and the idioms did not always translate smoothly. Linguistic difficulties aside, it was indisputable that the author was a deeply holy priest and a highly astute psychologist who tried to get to the roots of his own complexities by writing about them, turning his thoughts into paperbacks that, in turn, brought people closer to God and even helped transform their lives. But he wasn't only a writer. His electrifying performances as a preacher and teacher held audiences riveted, although it was sometimes difficult for them to believe that the intense and passionate Roman Catholic evangelist, waving a Bible from the pulpit or crashing into furniture as he clumsily crossed a stage, was the same, apparently contemplative, figure known to millions through his intimate discourses. Everyone I spoke to remarked on his presence, both on a platform and in person.

With a penchant for popularization, he united disciplines and embraced differing traditions. However, away from his frank writing, public charisma, and compassion to anyone in difficulty, Henri was privately stalked by demons that haunted him from playpen to grave. For anyone curious about the man behind the author, the physics of his personal pilgrimage remains endlessly fascinating. During a visit to New Mexico, not long before he died, he spoke of his attraction to the American painter Georgia O'Keeffe. He said that just as Vincent van Gogh's story and his paintings belonged together, so O'Keeffe's background and her art should be understood as a unity. The same is true of Henri Nouwen, whose entire life and work are of apiece and should be studied together.

Henri lived at a time that saw an increased fascination with mysticism. Not only was there an upsurge of scholarly interest in the Western and Eastern mystics—at university in the mid-1980s, I studied the Christian mystical tradition as a unit toward my final degree in Theology and Religious Studies—there was also a significant rise in the numbers practicing meditation and deeper states of consciousness. The first known treatise on mystical theology was written at the end of the fourth or beginning of the fifth century by an anonymous Syrian monk known as Dionysius the Areopagite. It took the form of practical instructions to a follower on climbing the mountain of prayer, leading him into a cloud of unknowing where, like Moses, he met God in impenetrable darkness. At the same time, the desert fathers and mothers of Egypt were helping people enter contemplative silence, their teachings often communicated through pithy sayings. These *abbas* and *ammas* were to make an impact on Western monasticism, but their main influence was on the Christianity of the East, where mystical theology flourished. The Hesychasts taught the Jesus Prayer ("Lord Jesus Christ, Son of God, have mercy on me, a sinner"), which struck a chord with Henri as its constant repetition was aimed at helping the praying person move from the mind to the heart. In the fourteenth century, mystics appeared in the Rhineland, Flanders, and in England, while, in sixteenth-century Spain, Carmelites, such as Sts. Teresa of Avila and John of the Cross, taught an ecstatic mysticism, guiding contemplatives through the dark night of the soul to the summit of Mount Carmel or through a series of rooms or "mansions" to the center of the interior castle.

Mystical or ascetical theology was taught in Roman Catholic seminaries and university theology faculties in the first half of the twentieth century as a pastoral discipline in helping students both to pray and guide the contemplatives they might meet in their future ministry. Henri would certainly have received instruction in Holland, but after the Second Vatican Council (1962–65), the subject, assumed old-fashioned and irrelevant, tended to be wiped from the curricula of Catholic foundations. William Johnston, a Jesuit priest and prolific writer on mysticism, believed mystical theology needed to be rewritten for the men and women in the twenty-first century, and, to a large degree, this is what the books of Henri Nouwen succeeded in achieving. Johnston said the subject should be restored to its "honored place" in theological studies but in a renewed, updated, and relevant format—again, Nouwen's writings certainly paved the way. "The challenge confronting us is to be true to the Gospel and tradition while facing the unique problems that have arisen in the twentieth century," writes Johnston.[3] Alas, he does not cite Nouwen, who harnessed Christian spirituality with psychology to speak to a global audience, some of whom were disenchanted with institutional religion but still longed for an experience of the divine.

The Jesuit scholar George Schner, a professor at Regis College, Toronto, where Henri had once taught spirituality, agreed that the pastoral theologian had earned a place in the field. His work would always find a niche in the Christian mystical tradition, but it was nonetheless independent of any specific theological movement, a timeless spirituality of the heart that would continue to survive and flourish. Henri Nouwen was writing ascetical theology in a popular vein and being more optimistic than some authors about the spiritual condition of modern culture. What marked him out was that he was a spiritual writer who, culturally and intellectually, was also a profound thinker. His education and early formation in Europe made his writings of particular interest to North Americans in terms of their philosophical, theological, and cultural analysis, avoiding the snares of being either too psychologically focused or cosseted in piety.

"Nouwen was attempting to do something which would survive in the long run in the great tradition of ascetical theology, reinventing the Christian tradition in an innovative way which was both appropriate for the times and succeeded in transmitting the essential message," said Professor Schner, who believed that, in order to understand what Nouwen succeeded in achieving, it was necessary to have invested to some degree in the cultural and intellectual background, as well as the depth of appreciation, that he possessed. Part of his gift was the dexterity with which he popularized and refashioned the mystical in such a way that it became accessible for a wide constituency. "It could have issued forth in technical books, but he carried on the great Catholic tradition of being intellectually astute and spiritually sensitive," Professor Schner enthused. "He had a flair for addressing young people, not by pandering to the currents of the day, but by teaching a rendition of mainstream Catholicism in a very pertinent, culturally critical and appropriate way."

Modern Western contemporary culture had closed off an established, easy access to the sense of the transcendent in the world that could be variously described as "the revelation of God, God's grace or the Holy touched." Other sciences such as psychology, sociology, philosophy, and theology had their merits, but if the heart, the inner person, the deepest part of the self, were not open to God, had no ears, eyes, or spiritual senses to find God, the rest was useless. Nouwen would never think of turning in popular material alone or selling out deep Christian principles and history to another science or discipline for novelty's sake. To some extent, he was stating the tried and true, but he always attempted to clothe it with the correct rhetoric, assess the audience and its needs, and "rediscover, in this closed environment, an opening to the transcendent."

But what do we mean by the word *mystic*—and how did Henri define it? Almost a century ago, the Anglican writer Evelyn Underhill was faced with a similar puzzle. In her *Mystics of the Church* (which Henri once pored over in a monastery), she states that "mystic" and "mysticism" are words "so vaguely and loosely used that they convey no precise meaning to our minds, and have now come to be perhaps the most ambiguous terms in the whole vocabulary of religion."[4] According to its historical and psychological definitions, Underhill says, "mysticism" is the direct intuition or experience of God,[5] while a "mystic" is someone who, to a greater or lesser degree, is given such a direct experience, a person whose life and religion are centered, not only on an accepted belief and practice, but also on firsthand knowledge.[6]

The word *mysticism* comes from the Greek and is derived from a root meaning "to close." The *mystae*, or mystics, were originally the initiates of the "mysteries," having an esoteric knowledge of "Things Divine" about which they had to remain silent. Later, mysticism came to mean closing the mind to external influences, so it could withdraw into itself and prepare to receive divine illumination. Mysticism, a key component of many of the world's religions, is regarded these days as an innate tendency of the human soul to transcend reason in order to have a direct experience of God. The aim of all mystics, then, is to attain a conscious relationship with the Absolute, desiring to know only that they may love.

In Underhill's judgment, the Christian mystic is one for whom God and Christ are not simply objects of belief, but living facts—experimentally known at firsthand—and mysticism becomes a life based on a conscious communion with God. Experience shows that, whatever form it takes, a mystical encounter is always a communion of love and "so intimate and all-pervading that the word 'union' describes it best."[7] In her other reflections, Underhill speaks also of the "consecrated loneliness" of the mystic who encounters the divine, not as a spiritual individualist, but as an ambassador of the human race. She also classes the mystic as a "creative artist."[8]

The contemporary theologian Ursula King defines a mystic as a person deeply aware of the powerful presence of the Divine Spirit, someone who seeks, above all, the knowledge and love of God, and who experiences to an extraordinary degree the profoundly personal encounter with the energy of Divine Life. She believes mystics often perceive the presence of God through nature and in all that is alive. This leads to a transfiguration of the ordinary all around them, but "the touch of God is most strongly felt deep within their own hearts."[9] Mystics offer a message of wholeness and healing, of harmony, peace, and joy, and of immense struggles fought and won. Many are drawn to them because they find their lives inspiring and their words transformational, especially at times when old values and certainties have broken down and when there is much spiritual hunger in the age of "the seeker." King points out that, for many Christian mystics of the past, the motivation was both an inner and outer quest, a journey that first led into the divine center of their own souls before moving outward again to the concerns of

God's created world and suffering humanity. It is certainly possible to see Henri Nouwen's life through this lens.

The Benedictine monk and international spiritual teacher Brother David Steindl-Rast, who was a friend of Henri, says we are all meant to be mystics. Understanding mysticism as the experience of communion with Ultimate Reality, he believes all of us are called to share in it, but it will be experienced differently by each of us, so we can only be a special kind of mystic in our own uniqueness. "We do a great disservice to mystics by putting them up on a pedestal and thinking of them as a special kind of human being," he writes. "The truth is that every human being is a special kind of mystic, and that creates a tremendous challenge for each one of us to become precisely that mystic we are meant to be."[10]

In the same way, Henri had no fancy ideas about whom he believed a mystic to be. In his book *In the Name of Jesus*, he states simply and unambiguously, "A mystic is a person whose identity is deeply rooted in God's first love." He explains that we have to be mystics if we want to live a life that is not dominated by the desire to be relevant but "safely anchored in the knowledge of God's first love."[11] Here lies the core of his teaching—and his own life of prayer: Our true self is in God and the spiritual life is coming into touch with that first love. "The mystical life is the life by which I grow toward what is real and away from illusion, the life that grows into true relationship. The future of Christianity in the West depends on our ability to live mystically, that is, in touch with that core reality which is at the center of events. Without claiming this truth that everything is in God, Christianity loses its transforming power and becomes something like 'behaving decently,' a series of rights and wrongs."[12] Spiritual discipline is about claiming our connected relationship with God and with one another—and living out of it.

Whether or not you ultimately agree that Henri was a Christian mystic, I hope this book will help you understand more about the spiritual and psychological character of a man whose complexities and ironies were as bewitching as his knowledge and gifts.

While Henri often encourages his readers to move from one spiritual polarity to another (such as the journey from loneliness to solitude, resentment to gratitude, fear to love, and so on), the writer's personal life had its own binaries. But it seems to me that instead of moving from one to the other, he held on to both as he traveled, say, from the academic to the contemplative, or from the mind to the heart. There are all kinds of other couplets and contradictions in the story of Henri Nouwen: Holland and America, exile and homecoming, restlessness and community, psychology and spirituality, responsibility and freedom, being and need, fame and privacy, joy and depression, alacrity and sullenness, ability and disability, extroversion and introspection—all of them operating within a wider theological framework of moving from the moral to the mystical.

In the garden of his Boston home one warm afternoon in the fall, Robert Jonas, a close friend of the priest, told me that Henri was always a nondualist. He resembled an icon where, in gazing at it, you can suddenly perceive or experience the wholeness of who you are and what life is. "Henri was iconic in that sense because he was so human: he was neurotic, he could be narcissistic, he could be selfish and resentful; and at the same time he could be such an incredible transmitter of light, of the divine presence in the world, the divine message and divine vision. He could be these things simultaneously. If the incarnation is the integration of the human and the divine, Henri was that integration very clearly. You couldn't miss his neurotic stuff and you also couldn't miss the light that was being transmitted."

1

INTIMACY AND DISTANCE

God hugs you. You are encircled by the arms of the mystery of God.

—Hildegard of Bingen

A polished, black, Italian marble sculpture, with large white veins, was a talking point in Henri Nouwen's office at Daybreak. He couldn't stop gazing at it, and sometimes he would touch the marble so that he could feel its form against his body. The work of a local sculptor, *Communion* consisted of two faces close to each other but separated by what Henri described as "an energy-filled emptiness." Yet there was also a unity about it. The bodies from which the faces emerged were joined in pregnant expectation. The sculpture was one but also two, long-lasting yet fragile. The work seemed full but at the same time vacant, eternal yet rooted in time.

Pleasing in appearance, the sculpture also symbolized something psychologically discomfiting for Henri. The marble faces spoke to him of "the great tension in my own life: the tension between a longing for closeness and a need to keep my distance."[1] Was he alluding to his life as an aging Roman Catholic priest who, like some celibates in ordained ministry, was desperately lonely and feared the future? Did he long for intimacy with another person but knew what the consequences would be? Was he referring to a well-documented friendship at L'Arche that had broken down and cast Henri into therapy as well as despair? Perhaps it was all of them. There is considerable evidence, both anecdotal and in his own writings, that as Henri got older, the more agitated he became about potential isolation in the years ahead. Father John Garvey, of St. Nicholas Albanian Orthodox Church in New York City, recalled one of his conversations with him: "He was worried about what would become of him when he grew old. We told him that we—and, of course, many of his other friends—would be happy to have him. 'Oh, no one will want a cranky old priest,' he said, only half-joking. I really think he never accepted fully the fact that a lot of people loved him."

This uncertainty about love and being loved ran through his life like a marble vein on his office sculpture. These insecurities had manifested themselves initially in his early years when the young Henri was discovered nervously charging around his playpen and incessantly asking his somewhat alarmed parents whether they loved him. It was in fact Henri's father, Professor Laurent Nouwen, who disclosed these details of his eldest son's proclivities to Peter Naus, a social psychologist. He trained at the University of Nijmegen with Henri and was a lifelong friend. He learned that no matter what Laurent and Maria Nouwen did to reassure their eldest son, the question persisted. In his books, Henri writes that his mother loved him unconditionally, so, as a child, he must have been seeking the constant approval of his father.

Henri, the eldest of four, was caring toward his siblings, Paul, Laurien, and Laurent. Paul told me that his typically Dutch father could be "very severe," a man who was known to scrutinize his children's career prospects. One of eleven children, Laurent Nouwen had, in fact, spent a few months in a Dominican seminary when he was younger but later trained to be a lawyer, eventually becoming a successful professor of tax law at the University of Nijmegen. Henri described his father as "very bright and able to function well in the world of competition." As the eldest of the children, Henri felt he had been programmed to believe that he had to be at least as good as his dad, and there was a lifelong competitiveness between them. When he started to study for the priesthood, his father even began to read theology books. When Henri went into psychology, his father decided to acquaint himself with that subject as well. On the one hand, Henri experienced his father as "a very loving person" but, on the other, felt "by the way that he questioned and challenged me, he was vying with me to have the last word on the subject."[2] This didn't happen with his siblings, which annoyed Henri, but he kept his feelings to himself because he did not think his father should be challenged. Henri's later study of Rembrandt's *The Return of the Prodigal Son*,[3] with its insights into homecoming and unconditional love, made him realize that, as a child, resentment had been festering within him, as it was with the elder son in the painting. Henri's relationship with his father was never far from the surface of his own adult anxieties. Yet, shortly before his death, Henri's father told me, "Henri was very proud of me and he would always try to impress me by saying 'I'm a great man, Father. I have been a success.' I was very proud of his success. He was a very devoted son but also very human. I miss him a lot. He had much of his mother in him—eager, always working."

Nouwen's parents, who cared immensely for all their four children and gave them opportunities for academic careers, later admitted they had raised Henri in accordance with the doctrine of a German doctor who had specified that the best way of coping with the grasping nature of young children was to restrict food and physical touch. This might have accounted not only for the fact that Henri was always hungry as a youngster but also, more pertinently, for their son's lifelong need of intimacy. But Chris Glaser, who was taught by Henri, remembered him telling the story differently: that, as a toddler, he had constantly reached out of his playpen to his mother or father passing by, wanting to be picked up, held, and hugged. Yet the child-rearing manuals of the time argued against always responding to a youngster's desires, lest they be spoiled, so his parents resisted their natural inclination. Henri felt this had damaged him in ways still experienced in later life. Chris Glaser told me, "I don't believe that it's a coincidence that one of his own personal favorites among his books on the spiritual life was the one titled *Reaching Out*.[4] Reaching out is what Henri did as a toddler and as an adult."

Whatever the origins of Henri's childhood loneliness, there was undoubtedly a struggle for him in the realm of intimacy, craving, and feeling connected. There was a strong attachment between mother and son, suggesting that almost from birth Henri felt a need for security, affection, and love that by far exceeded what could normally be provided for a child. No matter what the parents did, this need of Henri's could not be satisfied. There might also have been something early in Henri's life, outside the control of the mother or the father, that somehow threatened the parental bond, or something happened later in his life that disrupted what had originally been a solid relationship. Henri's lifelong restlessness could have been associated not only with his lack of certainty over being connected as a child but also with his doubts about being socially connected as he grew older. This might account for the way Henri tended to rush around, perhaps in a desperate attempt to convince himself that he was connected after all, and that people did like, approve of, and appreciate him. If he hadn't done this, he would probably have floundered.

As I indicated in *Wounded Prophet*, John Bowlby's Attachment Theory, one of the most significant theoretical developments in psychoanalysis since Freud, can help us in understanding the possible reasons for Henri's cravings, although it cannot account for all his behavioral patterns. The theory differentiates between "secure" and "insecure" attachment. A person who feels attached is safe and secure, but an insecurely attached child, such as Henri, usually feels intense love and dependency as well as a fear of rejection, irritability, and vigilance toward their attachment figure, usually the mother. A lack of security might create a desire to be close and a simultaneous determination to punish the attachment figure for the slightest sign of abandonment. While there is no evidence of such behavior in Henri's childhood, it is possible to detect an ambivalent insecurity in his adult relationships. Attachment patterns are triggered by separation or threatened separation from the attachment figure, and they can have profound implications for psychological development and psychopathology throughout a person's life cycle.[5]

The demon that Henri had to fight continually was the lack of assurance about being connected or, in other words, loved. He would start to lose the battle when he was overly sensitive to what his friends did or did not do, said or did not say, but also when he was hurrying around all over the place, refusing to decline lecture requests and working relentlessly. Friends speculated that, while his talks delighted many an audience, some of the motivation for giving them might not have been as altruistic as people had imagined and was, in fact, an expression of unrest. Henri knew that. When he was overly busy, he was keeping himself at a distance from the personal issues he needed to confront. However, in wrestling with this particular demon, he was giving expression to his unrest, while at the same time helping other people. That was the tragedy but also the strength of Henri's life, said Peter Naus, who often wondered if, in the case of any outstanding person, the greatness really lies in learning to live constructively with those demons that always seem to be oppressing. It's not that they ever disappear, he told me, but a person can learn to live with them in a way that neutralizes them as much as possible. As a psychologist himself, Henri understood what was happening. The issue was whether he was learning to live with the problem creatively.

But perhaps the explanations are not solely psychological but spiritual as well. Was the extraordinary child in the playpen actually feeling disconnected from the love of God that he had experienced in the womb before birth? We know that, in his fifties, Henri was captivated by words he heard from the lips of the Dominican priest Père Thomas Philippe, who cofounded L'Arche with Jean Vanier. Henri had always understood that the mystical life—entering into a unifying communion with God—was the highest reward of the moral life. The classical distinctions between the purifying way, the illuminating way, and the unifying way, as the three progressively higher levels of the spiritual life, reinforced this view. The mystical life had always been assumed by the Church to be the life of a rarefied group who managed to reach the prayer of total surrender. But according to what Père Thomas told Henri in a private meeting, the mystical life actually lies at the beginning of our existence and not only at its end. This is what Henri notes in his journal at the time:

> We are born in intimate communion with the God who created us in love. We belong to God from the moment of our conception. Our heart is that divine gift which allows us to trust not just God, but also our mother, our father, our family, ourselves, and the world. Père Thomas is convinced that very small children have a deep, intuitive knowledge of God, a knowledge of the heart, that sadly is often obscured and even suffocated by the many systems of thought we gradually cultivate. Handicapped people, who have such a limited ability to learn, can let their hearts speak easily and thus reveal a mystical life that for many intelligent people seems unreachable.[6]

Without doubt, Henri was one of those spiritually instinctive children whose constant need of reassurance might well have been related to a prenatal sense of God's love that seemed overshadowed or distant after birth. He learned from a young age that

God was real and Jesus was "very, very present." His innate sense of vocation to the priesthood, around the age of five, was not surprising, given that he insisted on saying Mass in the attic as a spiritual adventure game, while his friends were gallivanting about in a nearby wood as cowboys and Indians (though Henri did offer to take on the less popular role of an Indian if his friends agreed to be his altar acolytes back in the loft). Henri's maternal grandmother, a businesswoman who had a large department store, fostered his calling and even arranged for the store carpenter to build him a child-size altar, asking her seamstress to sew all the vestments needed to "play priest." By the time he was eight, Henri had converted the attic into a children's chapel where he aped the Eucharist, gave sermons to his parents and relatives, and, for his brothers and friends, devised a hierarchy of bishops, priests, and deacons, as well as servers. A selector for potential priests (in the Church of England) told me that, if such information were to emerge these days about a candidate for ordination, serious questions might be asked about their lure of power and fantasy at such an early age. But Henri's grandmother had no such inhibitions and evidently regarded the game as spiritual formation as she cheerfully provided the chalices and plates, and "gently introduced me to a life of prayer and encouraged me in a personal relationship with Jesus."[7]

Henri's younger brother, Paul, remembered vividly the little church under the eaves: "My parents, who got him the costumes, didn't tell him to go and play in the garden," he told me. "They were in favor of the feelings he had. He was a priest from the beginning and my parents knew this. It was always in his mind. I was the server and dressed like one. I was always sitting there, doing Mass, assisting him. He studied everything and he imitated it. It was a Catholic liturgy with bread and wine. He did it more and more every day between the ages of 10 and 12. In the beginning it was a play, but he became very serious. My parents never pushed Henri. If he wanted an altar and a Bible, and to say Mass on Sunday mornings while we all had to sit through it as he made a little speech, they let him. He had a very close harmony with my mother." Even when he was starting double figures, Henri could appear aghast when he discovered people did not love God or Jesus with the same intensity as he did. There was an intimacy, closeness, and directness with his relationship with God, as though his Creator were sitting in front of him. In later life, when God seemed more distant and even absent, the childhood memories of "playing priest" helped keep him rooted in faithfulness. Henri grew up into a devout but emotional boy as the tentacles of loneliness moved in. "Henri was very much on his own, thinking a lot," Paul said. "He didn't sleep very well and was always awake in his mind. That was a problem for my parents. Sometimes he would bang his head on the wall and they had to calm him down." As Henri moved into adolescence, he cultivated a slight inferiority complex because he wasn't practically minded or coordinated. "My father would say: 'Paul, you may drive the car. Henri can't do that. Paul, will you open the bottle of wine? Henri can't do that. He'll let it fall.' That was always a failing with Henri."

Consequently, from an early age, Henri may have felt different and perhaps alienated. He was also cross-eyed as a boy and mocked at school. Loneliness became his companion early in life. Unlike other family members drawn to business, he showed little acumen and only nonchalant interest. Desiring to amass a fortune was not turned into a bedside intercession at night. "He was on his own," explained Paul. "I got to a high position in business and worked hard to get that job. But Henri was always on his line to God. We realize when we are older that we are on our way to God but he had it when he was eight. Throughout his life, his heaviest cross was looking for company and being loved."

RISING STAR

Henri was so resolute about becoming a priest that he urged his parents to send him to a junior seminary when he was twelve.

In the end, they sensibly made him wait until he was eighteen. Although by this age Henri knew what it was like to feel apart, at college he was so liked and admired by the other seminarians, they elected him senior of the community, a representative who liaised with professors, bishops, and speakers. It wasn't long before he was a talking point around the clerical corridors. As his Uncle Anton, Dr. A. C. ("Toon") Ramselaar, was a monsignor and president of the minor seminary, there was already something of a charismatic presence about the young Henri. He also stood out because he was from a well-to-do family and his father was a distinguished lawyer. Most other seminarians were from more modest backgrounds, among them Louis ter Steeg, who recalled his friend's prowess: "I remember the year before ordination all the students had to address the community during Sunday service as a test of their capacity to preach. Harrie, as he was known, was by far the most impressive."

Most students in those days didn't travel far but at the age of twenty-one, it was suggested that Harrie (as he was known in Holland) go to Britain to improve his English. His host was Julian Wild, who, from a parish in Kisumu, Kenya, remembered him as "an unforgettable person." At the time, Julian had been studying in the seminary of the Mill Hill Missionaries in Roosendaal, Holland, and was asked if he could take a Dutch seminarian to his home in northeast England over the summer. That student turned out to be Harrie. Although Julian's colleagues in the Netherlands had not been greatly impressed by Harrie when they met him, Julian certainly was, and for two weeks entertained him at his small, terraced home in Easington, County Durham, a more working-class environment than he had ever been used to. Yet even then, his unrelenting restlessness came to the fore as he was keen to go everywhere and do everything. When Julian Wild's mother was baking, Harrie had to try his hand as well. Julian's sister kept rabbits, so Harrie had to learn about them as well. They visited many sights, including Durham Cathedral, and made a three-day pilgrimage to the Marian

Shrine of Walsingham in Norfolk. Harrie chatted to everyone on the bus and they all enjoyed his company. Even though he was then five years away from ordination, he was allowed to wear full clericals including a Roman collar. After all, if he had acted the priest as a child, it seemed only logical to do the same as a seminarian. One of Julian's relatives was the deputy manager of a coal mine, so they both had a conducted tour "down pit," where Harrie, always curious of people and their lives, set to work quizzing the miners. But according to Wild, "The local parish priest was not greatly impressed by him. He was a very reserved English gentleman, and Harrie was too pushy for his liking." However, Julian's mother paid Harrie the supreme accolade in the Durham dialect: "Aye, Harrie was a grand lad." Julian and Harrie kept in touch, Julian later spending a day with the Nouwen family at their larger home in The Hague. Later, Julian invited Harrie back to England again, but this time he couldn't accept as, ever inquisitive and proactive, he had already planned a visit to Kerry, Killarney, and Donegal in Ireland in the capacity as a student journalist—his first writing assignment. His articles were published in Dutch newspapers. Henri Nouwen's name started to be noticed at a young age.

With a capacity for creating community, Harrie got on well with people, but even in those days, Louis ter Steeg detected something else: "I noticed his craving for friendship and all the more so because there was always a kind of reservation in the seminary. It was a climate more of comradeship than real friendship. He would come along to have a talk to you on a very warm, friendly basis. He was able to demonstrate affection." But the climate of priestly formation in the 1950s forbade special friendships. Seminarians were expected to lead disciplined, holy lives, mistrusting the body and their own emotions. Intimacy was to be kept at a distance, a rule that ran contrary to Henri's already well-attuned sense of relationality.

By the time of his ordination in July 1957, the young, independently minded Father Nouwen had already negotiated a package with his bishop—the stories vary as to who asked whom—to embark on a seven-year study of psychology at the Catholic University of Nijmegen, followed by a course in the United States. It was certainly an unusual move for the era and inevitably set him apart from most of his seminarian friends, who were sent off without question to duller places as new priests. At a reunion of ex-seminarians in Holland not long before he died, Henri was reportedly (and not uncharacteristically) "terribly hurt" when former classmates rounded on him for having taken "the easy way out," leaving Holland at a time when the advance of secularism was testing the Dutch Church to the limit. In reality, his life was anything but easy, and he suffered from the narrow-minded resentment that can assault and stifle gifted people who, if they are to flourish in their uniqueness, need paths to be created for them.

Having been formed as a priest, Henri was eager to learn how people behaved, thought, and felt. He wanted to know what was going on in their inner lives. It was sometimes remarked about Henri that he always knew how to schmooze and move in the right circles, but it could also be said that he was simply as curious about powerful people as he was any other type. Nonetheless, when Henri had something in mind that he wanted to do, and he needed the connections to achieve it, he knew how to make them. For example, after steep criticism of the Roman Catholic Church's response to the Holocaust, he got involved in discussions between Jews in Israel and Roman Catholics in Holland. With his flair for making contacts, he met the Israeli ambassador to Holland, then organized meetings that dealt with tensions between Roman Catholics and Jews, all the while trying to work toward a deeper understanding of the State of Israel. "I think some people would say he was making a name for himself but that's not how I saw it," said Peter Naus. "I think he truly thought this was an important matter and he believed in the work that his uncle was doing. He tried to improve relationships between Roman Catholics and Jews." As well as being noted for his ecumenical work among Protestants,

Monsignor Ramselaar advised the pope on Jewish–Catholic relations, fighting for greater recognition of Israel by Rome and greater acknowledgment of the Holocaust. As youngsters, Henri and Paul had become highly attuned to the sensitivities of Christian–Jewish relations. They had lingering memories of the Gestapo driving through Dutch villages in their red Porsches and of their Jewish neighbors, including a famous blind pianist, being arrested and taken away to the concentration camps. "Our uncle took us to Israel many times to get the feeling of being together with the Jewish people," said Paul. "People said Henri and I actually looked like Jews and we were proud of that."

Father Jan ter Laak, another priest at the University of Nijmegen undertaking further study, remembered Henri as a nervous but inquisitive man in those days: "Seeing one person, his eyes were always going to another." As an open and progressive young priest in Holland, Henri always had people around him. Yet his influential background also set him apart, and there was always tension between him and other priests who had talents but weren't so popular as Henri in public. Whatever other people felt, Henri probably sensed he had a unique, universal mission in life that, at that time, was still unfolding. While he needed a larger map than the Netherlands, he suffered the resentment of others, not only because of his prestigious family background, but also because of his attractive difference, which was fundamental in motivating him to become a prophetic witness for the Christian Church. People who are talented and confident are often admired by their audience, be it students, parishioners, or readers, but they tend not always to be respected by many of their peers because envy and resentment kick in. They are always in danger of falling prey to envy when they prove popular with the masses but do not fit the traditional mold. At Nijmegen, Henri also ran into difficulties with his tutors. His plan to write a thesis on the American case study method was turned down by the psychology department, which requested a more clinical approach using quantitative data and analysis. Henri refused to be straightjacketed and withdrew his prospectus. He left the university with a doctorandus, a professional qualification, but not the doctoral research degree he wanted.

All this must have contributed to Henri's sense of isolation in his younger days when he also gained experience as an army chaplain and as chaplain for the Holland America line. A picture from the Nouwen family album shows him entering New York Harbor in 1962, wearing full clericals and a patterned scarf resembling a stole. He could never have realized the spiritual impact he was to make on the country, but he knew his first visit would not be his last. Henri needed courage to make a permanent move across the Atlantic in 1964—for more pioneering study. His father told me how much this had impressed him and how his son "went with nothing." Although tipped for greatness, the future world-renowned spiritual teacher clearly believed in the necessity of having a solid training behind him, and America (rather than the Netherlands) was patently the place for his innovative work.

2

THE INTERIOR CASTLE

It is foolish to think that we will enter heaven without entering into ourselves.

—Teresa of Avila

Henri Nouwen's psychological training in Kansas between 1964 and 1966 was one of the most significant periods of his life, as he learned to integrate his spiritual journey with his newly found psychological knowledge and understanding. It became the formational springboard for his teaching and writing ministry that was waiting in the wings. Henri won a fellowship in religion and psychiatry to study at the Menninger Foundation for Psychiatric Education and Research in Topeka. Its reputation had grown following the demand for psychiatrists to treat military veterans after the Second World War; eventually, it became the largest psychiatric training center in the world. A course in a largely Protestant institution on the other side of the world was a bold move for the ambitious young Catholic priest, but Henri sensed it was the right place for him at the time. Here he learned that, in the treatment of psychiatric patients, making the right diagnosis was the primary task of the healer.

Henri's neatly typed case study notes reveal a genuine desire for unity at many levels—a mystical approach in a psychiatric ward. Here we also see his ecumenical spirit forming. He laments the fact that, as a Catholic priest, his responsibility is limited to Catholic patients in the three wards he visits as part of the psychiatric team, while a Protestant chaplain meets a wider range of people from Southern Baptists to members of the Salvation Army. Ministers have care of an entire ward, he observes, while Catholic priests only look after the Catholics on the ward. The question frequently asked of him outside the hospital is how could he be both a priest and a psychologist if "religion contradicts psychology"? As for the therapeutic group process, Henri acknowledges that, in a certain way, the priest plays an unhealthy role: "He evokes sectarian feelings and stress by his presence, separation instead of union." Perhaps, here, Henri is thinking as an instinctive mystic as well as an aspiring ecumenist. The segregation confirms that Christian divisions are possibly never more offensive than in hospital settings. His role as a Catholic priest exiles him from the rest of the team. It is difficult for a priest who solely offers pastoral care to a minority group to be pastor of the whole ward because his therapeutic influence isn't allowed to develop. It is clear that he feels alone at different levels. Probably for the first time in his writing, he addresses a topic that was to preoccupy him for the rest of his life—anxiety. He states that what is certain about his work with "mental patients"—the term used then—is that it "aroused a lot of anxiety in me." It is only after some months that he finally realizes how much anxiety exists in his relationship with patients. Anxiety limits the capacity to hear, see, ask, or respond—in other words, to be receptive. It makes him self-centered and self-concerned, holding back authentic sympathy and empathy for others. Anxiety prevents him from noticing the real needs and learning from off-the-cuff remarks or opening questions. What is particularly noteworthy from these days, however, is his need to be affirmed—even by those patients he visits. He writes,

> I realize my preoccupation with the question in how far the patient likes you or not. To me this is one of the most frustrating preoccupations especially while the infantile quality of it is so obvious. It resulted sometimes in a too explicit attitude and an impatient reaction, a need to establish a personal intimate relationship as soon as possible, hereby sometimes forgetting how sick the patient was. So the anxiety limited also the capacity to see the patient as a patient exactly because anxiety reverses the process and makes the chaplain a patient who needs the other.

We see here, then, how his seminal thinking about the wounded healer and his personal experience in the hospital are evolving.

In psychiatric literature, mysticism and schizophrenia have often been linked, while some writers, including Freud and Menninger, have postulated that mystics demonstrate a special form of schizophrenia. Although there may be no direct correlation here, it is still worth recording that Nouwen makes a point in his notes of stating that neurotic or borderline schizophrenic patients and sociopathic patients seem more "attractive" to him than the severely depressed or chronic schizophrenics. These selection criteria "show very clearly how much projection and identification played a role in my pastoral concern. In fact, I had much contact with other patients, too, but they did not really concern me as much as these. In a way, I consider the possibility to identify with a patient as a positive trait."

When Henri arrived at Menninger as one of the first Roman Catholic priests to train there, he again felt different as he found himself among other ordained men of different Christian denominations, along with Jewish rabbis and psychiatrists. They had lively discussions about how the disciplines could meld, for the benefit of the Church and the world of psychiatry. "Henri represented the best combination in that he was able to combine those two dimensions better than anybody I knew," said Dr. John Dos Santos. "I'd seen others who became counsellors, clinicians, or therapists, and those who never did a good job of bringing it together. I always had the sense that Henri was someone who spoke like a counsellor and therapist, but at the same time, in terms of theology, what he said was professionally, therapeutically, relevant stuff." It was Dr. Dos Santos who brought him to the University of Notre Dame, at South Bend, Indiana, to help set up the program in pastoral theology. Once again, Henri stood out at Notre Dame for his *different* approach to psychology. Several members of the staff were trained in the more scientific school of classical behaviorism, which places strong emphasis on measuring people's behavioral patterns but tends to be distrustful of what is said about what is going on *inside* a person. Henri, however, placed a lot of emphasis on people's experience; it was the inner life that had to be known rather than a person's outer behavior. His psychology had been much influenced by some of his professors who were phenomenologists. They had focused on a person's experience, describing it in as much detail as possible and giving particular attention to the inner life. In many ways, Henri's evolving spirituality emerged from the psychology he had been exposed to, more than the other way around. From the outset, Henri opted for a pastoral rather than a scholarly approach to teaching. Eager to convey a knowledge of God that was real, simple, and direct, he wanted, as much as he could, to help students on their own journeys. Although intellectually astute, he never saw himself as an academic but as a pastor using the classroom as a pulpit. From the start, he understood his ministry as "laying down his life for one's friends," not as a literal form of physical martyrdom, but as someone who had sufficient self-knowledge, as advocated by St. Teresa of Avila in the first mansion of her interior castle, to offer his pain and confusion toward the healing and growth of others.

It must be acknowledged that Henri felt a degree of disconnection during his early years in the United States. Away from Holland and in a new culture, his need for friendship and community preoccupied his thoughts, while, at the same time, he was continually anxious about whether he would succeed in his chosen path. But he also came to own the fact that these very insecurities were part of the great human struggle. So, if he were in touch at a personal level with uncertainties within himself, as a teacher and writer he could put other people in touch with theirs. To put it in a more spiritual framework, he believed that, before announcing the good news, he had first to break the ground where healing could bear fruit. The Word of God needed fertile soil. Just as God stripped himself of power and Jesus did not cling to his equality with the Father, so, as a follower of Christ, Henri believed he had to offer his own bandaged wounds—that is, hurts that had been cared for—as a source of grace for others. His gift, therefore, was not his power but his willingness to be powerless and to trust that God's healing power would be made visible through that. Popular and respected among students, Henri found the work exhausting at times because so many people were drawn to him. Yet he would always go the extra mile to support anyone in need and, on one occasion, he gave particular support to a seminarian whose mental health issues had culminated in a depression. However, toward the end of his first year as professor of pastoral psychology at the University of Notre Dame, he too was in crisis. In May 1967, he visited Our Lady of Gethsemani Abbey in Kentucky, where, in some distress, he requested to see a brother, John Eudes Bamberger, who confirmed to me, "Henri was going through a difficult time in his life. He showed up at the guesthouse and asked if there was a monk he could talk to. When the guest master found out he was a professor of psychology, he thought someone with my own background as a physician would be appreciated. Obviously, I cannot and would not say what we discussed, but Henri felt it was very helpful and that was the beginning of our friendship. He came with considerable stress and crisis—and he left in peace." (On that visit, he also met another resident monk, Thomas Merton, his spiritual hero, a year before Merton's death).

Henri Nouwen dedicated his first book, *Intimacy*, to John Eudes. A series of essays in pastoral psychology, the text also reflects on questions that lie at the heart of the mystical quest: How can I find a creative and fulfilling intimacy in my relationship with God and my fellow human beings? How can one person develop a fruitful intimacy with another person? What does intimacy mean in the life of a celibate priest or in a community of religious? How can we be intimate with God during moments of celebration or silent prayer? Despite the private anxieties that were contributing at times toward a suffocating loneliness, he was still communicating "the unspeakable beauty of the divine" to his students.[1] As John Dos Santos put it, "What I recall is the holiness of the man and the almost magnetic effect he had on people—his ability to trust and for people to trust him. I have never met a saint before but he's as close as I ever got to one."

THE SPIRITUAL EXTROVERT

After a spell as a lonely teacher and supervisor back in Holland (on the one hand, he did not sense he was appreciated; on the other, he felt the odd man out in terms of the liberalizing tendency of the Dutch Church), Henri eventually returned to the United States to spend the next decade teaching at Yale Divinity School, his own style of communication honing gesticulation to fine dramatic art. The Quaker writer Parker Palmer noted that the "spiritual genius" possessed a peculiar awkwardness that almost became grace. The position of his hands and arms was almost grotesque but somehow, when you put it all together with his words, and the earnestness and passion of his presence, "it became quite beautiful in an astonishing way to watch him talk." As a teacher of pastoral theology in small or large groups, Professor Henri Nouwen commanded attention. There was something about him that was entrancing—and for some it was always at the level of mystery. He tended to get carried away with his subject. The passion bore him aloft and he lost himself in it. He spoke to the hidden places in people's lives where they felt most vulnerable and least capable—and somehow dignified them. He helped them see that it was precisely there that God wanted to meet them, touch them, and heal them. This was their divinely given, unique gift into their own spiritual life. Sometimes, however, his material could evoke hostility. The theme of ascetical self-denial, for example, was not easy for students to comprehend, and they tended to respond automatically with a psychological set of assumptions. To them, talking about self-denial and then commending it, in the way their mystical teacher did, sounded like a form of self-negation and self-rejection. Some of those training for ministry at the divinity school were wrestling with issues of self-esteem, so it might have sounded like Henri was asking them to beat up on themselves in a way that was psychologically untenable. Such situations could produce the occasional eruption in class with students registering a collective anger. If he felt he had been misunderstood, Henri would be patient as he explained his points again and would take time to meet students privately if necessary. One student, apparently disenchanted with his life, always remembered Henri pulling up his chair in front of him and focusing all his energy face-to-face so that he felt as though he were the only person in the world. The young man had never known such rapt attention. Henri intuited that, through their awkwardness, outbursts, or resistance, the difficult students might, in fact, be expressing a latent pain. While chatting to a student in his office, a chance remark about all the books Henri had on his bookshelves made him question whether the sight of so much learning might be intimidating students, making them feel they would never be able to compete with their professor. In the end, Henri decided to remove all his books and store them elsewhere.

As a marker, Henri was fair and never ruthless. He took the view that it was possible to evaluate work beyond strictly academic criteria. He expected good thinking and would reward that, but he could also see that, even if a paper wasn't particularly well written, there might still be an important new insight in it. He was also sensitive to the fact that, even though they had struggled with a course, some students might have really "given themselves" to the topic and come to a new place in their own lives. Henri would be keen to recognize that in the grade he gave. He was always looking into the heart and trying to reflect in his assessment the kind of engagement he felt the student was having with the material. Henri was remarkably accessible to students. When he lived on campus in a student apartment, he left his door unlocked so people would never have to wait outside. In fact, anyone was welcome to enter and enjoy his home whether he was there or not. He invited students to pray with him in his apartment early in the morning and offered an evening Eucharist in the prayer chapel for students of any denomination. He was also the rare faculty member who attended social events for students and was often the life and soul of the party. Chris Glaser remembered the evening Henri led a big circle dance during a student party that featured a DJ playing pop music and kegs of free beer. He was invariably popular and had a generous spirit. "Every seat in the large lecture hall was filled for his own classes because he fed the spiritual hunger of students," he said, "and he was the only professor I knew to audit other professors' classes."

While Jim Forest was visiting from Holland, he learned that Henri had invited his students to an end-of-semester celebration. Many turned up. Then, at a certain point during the evening, he handed out booklets of psalms, saying, "Well, it's time to pray." There was a tremendous sense of nervousness in the room. Nobody was expecting a spiritual interlude to a party, but Henri achieved the transition in a most matter-of-fact way. "I thought this was real hospitality," Jim recalled. "He was not just giving them potato crisps and CocaCola: he was giving them his life—and me too. It was a very remarkable moment. Everybody afterwards probably decided, as I did, that it was the best thing about being there. We prayed together. There was this contagious enthusiasm about Henri that you couldn't be untouched by, no matter how you were feeling."

In terms of his literary output, Henri Nouwen was starting to make a name for himself as his teaching notes were turned into bestsellers with the careful and conscientious support of his teaching assistant, John Mogabgab. While the divinity school board was more used to its academics publishing scholarly articles on the medieval mystics or undertaking historical reviews, Henri shamelessly explored themes of the heart and the mind in such an accessible way that they were even likened to Kierkegaard's "edifying discourses," effecting something in the readers who would find themselves thinking along with the writer and even reading aloud his words. Books such as *Creative Ministry*, *With Open Hands*, *Reaching Out*, and *The Wounded Healer* were published during the early seventies, and readers couldn't seem to get enough of them. Standing out in his field, Henri was referenced in all kinds of publications. "His writings touched people deeply, and they were up-built by them. I don't think he had any peers in that regard," said Margaret Farley, who joined the divinity school staff on the same day as Henri. Both were the first Roman Catholic appointments there. "Not all of his works were equally powerful to everyone. He was always working out his own questions, his own search, which was, in fact, his own power—maybe the center of the power of his writings. Some books were so much his working-out that they appealed primarily only to people who were working out the same things. These didn't have the universal appeal that some of his other writings did. But overall I think his corpus is beyond compare."

The author's paperbacks began to be consumed by Protestants with a fervor that no Catholic writer like him had been read in centuries. The Protestant churches were at a point in their history when they really needed someone like Henri Nouwen. There was something fermenting, according to Margaret Farley, and it was related to a hunger for something more than the cerebral, more than preaching—a thirst for ritual as well as for wisdom and guidance in relation to their spiritual lives. Henri was able to speak to all that, and he managed it in view of his general power in being able to address anyone, but especially Christians. There was nothing parochial in Henri's Catholicism. He wasn't churchy but, as a Dutchman writing in simple English, he acquired a language for humanity. He was never apologetic but his was never a general spirituality. It was christocentric and trinitarian—all of it belonging at the heart of the *particularity* of Christianity and deepening the Catholic tradition. Henri didn't label or speak in ways accessible only to Catholics; indeed, much of the time people didn't realize that his words had been formulated in a deeply Catholic tradition. They just came across as profoundly Christian. This was how Henri succeeded in transcending denominational barriers. As Margaret Farley interpreted it, Henri Nouwen's message was "God is present. God welcomes us. We have a tremendous struggle even to believe that and find our way to God. Along the way, we need others who will join us in our journey." She added that Henri's personality was almost too powerful for himself at times. But his approach was always aesthetic as well as inspirational and spiritual. He came at the right time for the churches. It was the dawn of a new openness that Henri brought to a fullness of time.

When Marjorie Thompson was a Master of Divinity student at McCormick Seminary in Chicago, Henri came over from Yale to lead a quiet day retreat. As soon as he began to speak, Marjorie knew she was experiencing something she had not received in her own Presbyterian tradition at any time in her life—the sense of quiet, the comfort level with silence, and a different, reflective approach to God's Word. "In what he shared with the community, I saw what I felt I had been missing in my own seminary experience," she remembered. "One could tell in Henri's presence that he was a man steeped in prayer and that he had a deep, quiet core of life with God. This shone through everything he did. It was reflected in his presence and in how he led that quiet day—that was part of what helped me recognize what I had been missing. It was very rare to find that sense of presence in a person," she said. Henri had seemed centered and his words had been economical. She felt Henri appealed to Protestants because he always spoke directly to the heart. His genius was in his taking something of his own experience and struggles of the spiritual life and articulating them in such a way that made them universally accessible. That was why Protestants and Catholics alike responded to him. He had an ability to speak of the spiritual life in ways that transcended the particularities of the Roman Catholic tradition, even though he was well rooted and grounded there, so much so that Protestants were comfortable reading and finding their own experience reflected in his words. Later, as a research fellow at Yale Divinity School, Marjorie Thompson audited Henri's courses within the framework of her own independent study. She observed how he was always coherent about what he was keen to convey, using simple images and words in his lectures and seminars. In the midst of all the gesturing, there was a "tremendous focus" on what he was communicating and "in that, lay a sense of his centerdness and what was at his core." He managed to hold his inner and outer life together, feeling the necessary tension between being engaged with the issues of the world and having sufficient time to attend to his own spiritual life.

Henri's charismatic power seemed to radiate with remarkably good timing. Local hospice nurse Mary Carney was taking care of leukemia patients, many of whom were dying at tragically young ages. She happened to be attending a conference when she heard him speaking on "care for the caregivers." She had no idea who he was, but his talk came at the right time. "It struck an incredible chord with me and, after hearing him speak, I walked for two hours," she said. Like others caring for the dying, Mary felt she needed support. Such was the emotional strain of their work; most of those she was working with were having difficulty going to church without crying. Mary Carney eventually met Henri at the divinity school when he was involved in theological reflection on chaplaincy work. She would also join him in the chapel for his engaging Masses. "It was the first time I was able to be in church and participate without being overwhelmed by what I had experienced during the day," she explained. "I observed him. I was Irish and cynical so I looked at this bright guy, disbelieving that he could be as sincere as he was. I think we became good friends because I laughed at his jokes. Many people with troubles stayed after Mass and just wanted to talk to him. He was so focused with them. I was really taken aback at his manner. I became intrigued by this person. He was very grateful for people listening to what he had to say. I think he really appreciated this continuum of engagement after his sermons. He never expected people to remain connected to him. He didn't really believe people liked him as much as they did. I knew very well that, when he heard the stories people were telling him, he actually *heard* and *experienced* deeply what they were saying. He really prayed about it. He *felt*. His intuitive sense was strong. He could go into a room and almost fine-tune to the person who needed to be heard." Mary's father had been the janitor at Yale, and although she didn't know Henri well at the time, Henri made a point of asking, after her father's death, whether she would like to have a Mass said for him at Yale. When Mary's mother died, Henri was away at the time, yet somehow especially present: "He just made a simple call. It was Easter Sunday and I had a sense he prayed her through. She received communion and died instantly."

Across North America and beyond, the fame of this holy man from Holland was spreading as he impacted people's lives in striking ways. So what was it about him? For an answer, I turned to Raymond Tomkinson, a British priest and author, who said the task of all pastoral theologians was to help people make connections between what was believed about God and how they should live. Although they could take a moral perspective—how people behave in relation to God and their neighbor—they could also reflect "the stance of the mystic who beholds—from within the gritty reality of human life—the presence of God." In *The Wounded Healer*, Henri Nouwen asserts that "the mystical way is the inner way."[2] In his book *Life Shaping Spirituality*,[3] Raymond Tomkinson discusses both the inward and the outward spiritual course, suggesting that some people find one or other journey easier to make. Much depends on personality. There is some correlation between introversion and extroversion in terms of the inward and outward journeys, but it would be erroneous to assume that only introverts could make the inner journey or that only introverts could be mystics. Indeed, Henri was a strong extrovert.

Raymond Tomkinson thinks the distinction can be tested in relation to the common human experience of loneliness. The mystic is acutely aware of loneliness because mystics know their spiritual home to be in God: in the heart of the community of the Holy Trinity. Loneliness, for the mystic, is actually homesickness. The only real difference between a mystic and anyone else (including those who have not yet discovered the mystic within) is that the mystic has named the loneliness for what it is: the illusion of being alone, experienced negatively. What mystics seek to do is to acknowledge the phenomenon, to behold it, and to embrace it as a necessary experience this side of heaven. It is a consequence of exploring an encounter with God. The more we are in love with God, the more acutely we feel separated from the Divine Lover. At least, he says, that is what it seems like. The truth is that we are never alone. The more we allow ourselves to be drawn into the heart of God, the more we are aware of our alienation from God and the tension between the two is not a hard wire that binds us, more a circus tightrope that we learn to walk with care and patience.

It might be asserted that the "introvert mystics" cope better with loneliness than the "extrovert mystics" because they draw their energy from meeting God in an "aloneness" inside them. Extroverts, like Henri, draw their spiritual energy from people around them, and can feel isolated and enervated if left to their own devices even for a short time. However, what they know, instinctively, is that all human life—indeed, all creation—is one, that we are all connected one to another. They are good at making that clear by the way they come to life in the company of friends or strangers, as Henri always did. Thus, the extrovert mystic reminds us of the participation of all creation in the Divine Life. "Henri Nouwen was an excellent example of the well-balanced mystic," said Raymond Tomkinson. "He trod the inward and the outward journey, coming to know the pain and the joy of both— the paradox of knowing we are never alone, yet sharing deeply in humanity's unconscious sense of alienation."

3

DEPTH AND BREADTH

*Our task is to listen to the news that is always arriving out
of silence.*

—Rainer Maria Rilke

Hammering chunky nails into solid oak beams, rolling heavy
boulders, rummaging for small stones in a tub of raisins, and
handling hot pans in the bakery were not disciplines that came
naturally to the forty-two-year-old "novice." He was not accustomed
to long and weary shifts, such as mechanically placing dough on
troughs, taking the raisin, white grain, and sunflower loaves out of
the ovens and laboriously packing them—one after the other. The
other monks could see the newcomer at the Abbey of the Genesee
wasn't cut out for their life, but, nevertheless, they couldn't help
but admire his effort and commitment. "His beauty was that he
got involved with virtually anything—even raisin washing," said
Brother Christian. "If raisin washing was what God had asked him
to do, boy he was going to do a good job." Henri was amazed at
all that went on at the Trappist monastery in upstate New York,
including the regular collection of medicines from a pharmacy

or going to a medical center to get specially made insoles for a brother with bad feet.

Wherever he walked, Henri Nouwen sent out signals of nervous energy during his first sabbatical there. His confinement within the enclosure and the need to remain silent tested his personality to the limit. His sensitivity, too, came under check when he wasn't thick-skinned enough to deal with monks who kidded him too much, picked on him, or made fun of his Dutch accent. This was one place where he couldn't do his own thing or jump in the car if it all became too much. "I think he was too much of a perceptive person," Brother Christian told me. "After he had been here a while, it was suggested that he should not read in the library, where monks were moving in and out, but go to his own room and get into the solitude within the four walls."

Brother Christian went on, "No man is a saint in the eyes of his valet," explaining that he had once asked Henri, "Where do you get all these beautiful thoughts that you are putting in the books because you don't come across like that in person?" Henri replied, "You know, Brother Christian, at given moments I read my own writings and think 'Did I write that?'" Then the monk acknowledged very seriously, "If you gave him a Bible, he was away, page after page. Writing was just a gift."

Kevin Bushe, a monastic family brother from Donegal, Ireland, noticed that Henri could be moody. "He could get quite down on himself for short periods, but then he snapped out of it very fast. Artists have that habit. He was a strong-minded person, intense and excited. Exhausting. Henri was a typical artist who took things seriously—too seriously sometimes. But I found him industrious, joyful, and congenial. He would answer any question and dialogue about anything. I was a carpenter, so we sometimes talked about wood, how cedars symbolized eternal life and how soft wood doesn't rot in the rain or bad weather. I told him to ponder the Spirit more and let him direct his thoughts instead of agonizing. He said I was right."

While never a call to a monastic profession, living as a brother and sharing their physical and spiritual life allowed Henri to enter into a new rhythm, aligning him with the contemplative dimension of Christian living as never before. He rose at 2 a.m. and was in bed by 7 p.m. He learned a new way of perceiving time and experiencing the presence of God. From his diary, it is evident that he was alert to "the mystical" during that period. For example, after the abbot, John Eudes Bamberger, gave a talk on the Holy Trinity, Henri specifically notes he was "clear, succinct, mystical, and extremely practical." What impresses him most is the simple idea that the praise of God is the criterion of the Benedictine life, and he comes to value the powerful implications of living for the glory of God: that it is in a loving community that God's glory becomes visible, and that by participating in the life of God, the brothers will always discover more of God's mystery in each other. At the monastery, Henri is naturally drawn to classical spiritual literature such as *The Ladder of Divine Ascent* by John Climacus, the most popular book in Eastern monasteries. His study of Evagrius, who wrote on the seven deadly sins, allows him to see anger as a serious obstacle to the spiritual life, while Dorotheus of Gaza helps him face his hurts and resentments. He also takes advantage of reading the library copy of Evelyn Underhill's *The Mystics of the Church*, in which she discusses the main mystical figures in the Western Church, showing how, after living through the most ecstatic experiences, the mystics are "frequently capable of unbelievable activity." St. Paul is the prime example, along with Sts. Augustine, Teresa of Avila, and Catherine of Siena. "Mysticism," he notes, "is the opposite of withdrawal." Intimate union with God leads to the most creative involvement in the contemporary world as ecstasies and visions are slowly replaced by a "steady inward certainty of union with God and by a new strength and endurance." Although frequently experiencing "sudden waves of fervent feelings" in this often-active period, the mystic is "nonetheless calm and sober in his practical dealings with men."[1]

In terms of his own inner development, Henri needed to find a contemplative way of harnessing the psychological with the spiritual. On the one hand, he was highly sensitive to various dimensions of personal relationships; on the other, he had an authentic commitment to spiritual values. To survive, he had to bring them together somehow. It was by trying to remain faithful both to his principles as well as to uncomfortable, relational situations that he came to understand both better. Working on them with persistence, and repeatedly going back to them time and again, he gradually modified some of the demands he put on himself as well as his reactions to people. It was a dialectical process, but he gained more insight as time went on. "Everybody has to do that same thing," said the abbot. "It's just that Henri did it with an intensity of feeling and an ability of expression that I think is limited to relatively few people. I think the reason he came to the monastery was that the spiritual dimension of his psychological life became more prominent, more urgent for him, as he went on with his priesthood. The psychological and social psychological had a great impact on ministry and on spirituality. He came to the monastery for integration."

Henri's chief source of suffering was found in his struggles to be less involved in his own emotional reactions to situations and people. He reacted very intensely and deeply—and not always with the poise that people require to function on a professional level. His saving grace was that he was in touch with this weakness of character and took responsibility for it. According to John Eudes Bamberger, "Henri was hurt by all kinds of small things. We were quite different people—psychiatry and psychology often don't quite meet. Psychology is much more theoretical. I was a physician. I was formed in that. I'm a monk and lived a very different lifestyle. I found it easy to like Henri. He was a very amiable person. I felt that part of Henri's suffering was that he was too sensitive in certain ways and let himself be hurt too readily by people. Some people, I guess, are born more that way. Henri came from a very high-powered environment, and I would presume that it was tied in with the way he was raised. If you're the son of the queen's economic adviser, you are probably going to have a very, very high demand for performance of you and that makes people very sensitive. It also made him very fruitful and often very perceptive but I suspect that was a big part of it."

Although Henri never had any serious plans of becoming a Trappist, except fleetingly once, his stay bore some semblance to a novitiate. With the intuitive and patient support of the abbot, it proved to be a time of deep spiritual formation. His struggles were not unique, but he came to terms with them and had strategies for dealing with them. The mystical side of his personality was nurtured, and he returned to teaching a more harmonious person. He reached a point of acknowledging the stark difference between his fast way of life in the university world and the more measured pace at the Genesee (which means "Beautiful Banks" in the native Seneca Indian language). Before resuming his teaching duties at Yale, he asked the abbot if he should wear his monastic habit on campus as a symbol of his association with the brothers, but was advised to return "as himself." Nevertheless, he took with him a copy of the monks' large, calligraphic psalter and kept it on a lectern in his room, inviting friends to pray with him from this elegant Book of the Psalms, the prayers of the heart. Henri once said that if he ended up in a prison cell rather than a monastic cell, and could take only one book, it would be a psalter.

Ever a journalist of the spiritual, Henri must have sensed that the journal he wrote up every day might be turned into a paperback, but he referred to *The Genesee Diary* as "this risky book," for it was the first time his own life had become the subject of his writing. In his previous publications, he had been, to some extent, a distant author. This, though, was his first intimate journal in which he was revealing himself. He need not have been apprehensive. It proved an outstanding success and was especially welcomed by Protestant ministers, drawn to the mystical. From that time on, the modern spiritual master entered a different category of renown. Invitations to speak came streaming in and he was more in demand than ever.

Robert Durback, a former Trappist monk who became a friend of Henri after he left Mempkin Abbey in South Carolina, was always surprised the author could manage to maintain a discipline of any sort in view of the way he seemed to be "devoured by people." There were more men and women taking advantage of his generosity than he could handle. "When I visited him the first time at Yale, I was impressed by the simplicity of his living quarters off campus, but then he took me to a small niche between two rooms," Robert told me. "There had been a water closet there but he had asked for it to be removed so he could place a priedieu, a wooden prayer desk where he kneeled. I could never have confined myself to such a crowded corner but Henri would spend a long time in prayer there. I don't know where he found the time to pray. But he didn't just talk about prayer, he spent time in it. It was a very intensive part of his life. The reason why he could be so active is because he carried this depth around with him."

Robert Durback had always intuited from Henri's writings that he spoke "the language of a monk and that there was already a lot of the monk in him." He could, in fact, write solid monastic spirituality. His emphasis on solitude and silence, and the value of these disciplines for the life of prayer, resonated with all Robert had been taught during his monastic years. "He had this penetrating insight into what really mattered, what was really at the heart of spirituality. For Henri Nouwen, every person was the place where he found God. It was clear that he reverenced every human being he was in touch with." He remembered sitting with Henri in the cafeteria at Yale and discovering how he was such a generous person. A student told him about his friend at the university who wanted to do a course but didn't have the money for it. "Don't worry," Henri replied, "I'll take care of that." Robert continued, "Henri paid for all my hospitality at Yale and, on the way back to the airport, even offered to pay my fare because I had gone to visit him. He wasn't just being humanitarian. Knowing all that went into Henri Nouwen, he had this tremendous sense of the presence of God in every human being." Robert Durback sat in on some of Henri's lectures and recalled his telling the students that, when they became pastors, they should not use phrases like "psychotic" or "neurotic" when describing parishioners. "You are dealing with human beings," he explained. "Do not use labels. They don't tell you the truth about people. The truth is that you have a human being here and you should respect that human being. Labels are not helpful in evaluating people."

Robert also spoke to me about the closeness he felt to Henri Nouwen as a spiritual writer:

> As a reader, I open his books, lay my head on them, and absorb them by osmosis. I am never in a hurry to get to the next page, and sometimes I spend a long time just with one paragraph. The very act of taking the time to read is *lectio divina*. It isn't just that I am admiring Henri Nouwen. I am aware that I am in the presence of God. Henri Nouwen's writing facilitates my personal union with God because he shares his own sense of communion with God. I simply assimilate his words and adapt them to my own personal needs.

CONTEMPLATION AND RESISTANCE

While Henri Nouwen might have been accused by the more cynical of being something of a dilettante, always on the lookout for a new theological experiment to test and turn into a book, he was always an authentic searcher in terms of his vocation. He knew that God could call you to different contexts, but it was only through prayer that they were discernible. His missionary spell in South America arose directly from his deepening contemplative life with the Trappists and was, in fact, one he had been seriously ruminating over for a decade or more. It was undoubtedly galvanized after he had the opportunity not only to meet but also to enter into a public dialogue with Dom Helder Camara, the Brazilian archbishop noted for his social and political work for the poor during the military regime. Henri, the priest from the affluent First World, relentlessly questioned the Third World liberation priest in Washington, DC, but sensed that there were truths to uncover only among the despised and rejected of the Third World.[2]

In October 1981, Henri left for Bolivia and Peru. One of those who admired his zeal was Father Gustavo Gutiérrez, a Peruvian priest and the founding father of liberation theology, who lived and worked among the poor of Rimac, a slum area of Lima. Faith and starvation should not coexist, believed Gutiérrez, because the God of Jesus is the God of life—of all life. God was a mystery, the love that embraced all. From him, Henri learned about the two forms of poverty—what he termed "a scandalous state" and "a spiritual childhood." The first was abhorred by God; the second valued. Each was present in Latin America where people hungered both for bread and for God. Liberation theology prioritized the gift of life as the supreme manifestation of God. Being poor was not simply lacking the economic resources for development but moreover a way of living, thinking, loving, praying, believing, and waiting.

In his journal, ¡Gracias!, Henri is attentive to the contemplative or mystical in all he experiences among the poor. Despite the appalling conditions of poverty around him, he is struck primarily by the concept of gratitude. While he longs to give the people food, housing, education, and employment, he realizes he is receiving hidden insights and skills from the people themselves. Gratitude is an intimate participation in the Divine Life itself. The way he sees God in others is a spiritual sensitivity enabling him to receive his neighbor as a messenger from God. The God encountered in prayer leads to a recognition of "the God among us." Gratitude is receiving God in and through the human interaction of ministry. "This viewpoint explains why true ministers, true missionaries, are always also contemplatives. Seeing God in the world and making him visible to each other is the core of ministry as well as the core of the contemplative life."[3]

As Henri explores a Carmelite convent chapel, he spies statues of Sts. Teresa of Avila and Thérèse of Lisieux, and he feels as though the two women are communicating with him as never before. On the Feast of St. John of the Cross, he writes that the sixteenth-century Spanish mystic speaks to him with great power. Not only did he face oppression, humiliation, and imprisonment as he attempted to reform the Carmelite order, but in the midst of his agony, he experienced God's love as a purifying flame, which found expression in his profound mystical poetry:

> St. John reveals the intimate connection between resistance and contemplation. He reminds us that true resistance against the powers of destruction can be a lifelong commitment only when it is fed by an ardent love for the God of justice and peace. The ultimate goal of true resistance is not simply to do away with poverty, injustice and oppression, but to make visible the all-restoring love of God. The true mystic always searches for this Divine knowledge in the midst of darkness.[4]

Henri notes that John of the Cross sings "the Song of the Soul Delighted by the Knowledge of God" even though "it is night." Right in the middle of darkness, the mystic sings of a light too bright for eyes to see. "In this divine Light, we find the source of our whole being. In this Light we live, even when we cannot grasp it. This Light sets us free to resist all evil and to be faithful in the darkness, always waiting for the day in which God's presence will be revealed to us in all its glory."[5] Here, then, Henri Nouwen, the world-class wanderer, is now writing as a more perceptive

Christian mystic. The struggle for liberation can, in fact, lead to an experience of great darkness, but this, in turn, results in true humility, which empowers people to continue the struggle. Henri sees deep connections between this understanding of humility and the humility of St. John of the Cross who stayed faithful in the darkness. The new spirituality of liberation "opens us to the mystical life as an essential part of the pastoral task given to us by the people themselves."[6]

It is worth bearing in mind that in *The Wounded Healer*, published a few years before, Henri had explained that it was his growing conviction that in Jesus the mystical and the revolutionary ways were not opposites, but two sides of the same human mode of experiential transcendence: "Every real revolutionary is challenged to be a mystic at heart, and he who walks the mystical way is called to unmask the illusory quality of human society. Mysticism and revolution are two aspects of the same attempt to bring about radical change."[7]

After South America came a *revoltus*, a "turning around," of Henri's own vocation. He felt that if he really had any calling in Latin America, it was to receive from the people the gifts they had to offer and convey them to North America for their own conversion and healing. Henri told me that he had gone to South America with the thought that he might spend the rest of his life there: "I had a very, very important time there. I learned Spanish, I worked with poor people and I learned. But I also learned that I shouldn't stay there. When I came back, people felt I should be a voice for Latin America in Northern America. That was a positive way of thinking about it. A negative way was that I found it hard. I didn't feel called there. I didn't feel that the Church in Latin America or even the people were saying 'yes, Henri we need you.' Latin America was more about *my* desire to go there. There was a lot of personal ambition—spiritual ambition—to do it. But I very soon found out that I wasn't made for that or that God didn't call me there and that the people didn't call me there. But it was not something I would have liked to miss."

It was, in fact, Gustavo Gutiérrez who made clear to Henri that his long-term place was not in Peru. He told him to go back to Harvard and claim the university as a platform from which to talk to the United States—no small order, it must be said. Taking up a position created for him, Henri taught at Harvard Divinity School and kept before him this mandate of "reverse mission"—to tell the First World not only about the problems that the Latin Americans were facing but also of their great faith, hope, and renewal of spiritual life that was taking place amid all forms of suffering. This was a mystic in action, trying to influence American society and even public policy concerning Latin America. There was a strong Third World orientation in Henri's mind. During one semester break, in a move to allow students "to fly," he sent a group to Haiti, a brainstorm of an idea and one he didn't think through practically. By the standards of Harvard Divinity School, Henri's approach to teaching was, to say the least, unusual. He tended to move people through different emotions while addressing issues that were welling up from deep inside him. It seems he rather dismissed the traditional methods of mystical thinking, telling the students, "If you go to seminary, they will tell you there are the three ways—*the via purgativa, the via illuminativa and the via unitiva.* Forget these stages—you'll never get to the unitive stage." It was more a question of students finding their own approaches. If he had a group of young people in front of him for half an hour, he was going to convey as much as he could about the range of possibilities that lay before them.

His zaniness at Harvard may have resulted from a sense of outer and inner displacement. He was looking for somewhere to pitch his tent and swiftly deduced that Harvard was not the place. The critical, intellectual atmosphere of the divinity school neither responded too kindly to guru figures, nor supported the kind of openness that Henri needed and thrived on. So academically involved were students in a hermeneutic of suspicion that they looked on Henri as someone else to be feared, accusing him of being a spiritual imperialist, someone with his own planned program of spirituality for others. In his second year, Henri made a point of trying to be more Christian, but this only augmented the tension. This was not his world nor his vision. The academic milieu was not his only struggle at the time. Organically, Henri was in depression, needing to be taken on walks and being encouraged to pray more. In his insatiable need for close friendship, he had a tendency to befriend young scholars and could be overwhelming in his neediness, a pattern of behavior that would come to a head in a matter of years. "What he did was turn this drive for intimacy, this terrible hunger for intimacy, into a whole new kind of spiritual life," a former colleague explained. "This was very much in keeping with the Western spiritual tradition. If you look at the lives of some of the great mystics, they had that same kind of intense, erotic need which was not met anywhere, was sublimated, and was part of their search for God. But I wouldn't want to reduce Henri's problems to the fact that he was a priest. The priesthood was, in many ways, made for Henri."

What most impressed administrative assistant Peter Weiskel was Henri's ability to break down barriers between people, and working with him was "an incredible experience of diversity." At his home, The Carriage House, it was not unusual to run into Russian Orthodox priests and monks, right-wing Christians, Latin American missionaries, liberation theologians, Liberal Protestants, Jews, and an occasional Marxist-Leninist for good measure. When the assistants of Charles Colson—the evangelical Christian leader who had served as special counsel to President Richard Nixon— walked in and saw some of the icons Henri had on his walls, they "literally jumped as if they might be haunted, something that was so utterly out of their experience they didn't know what to do. Yet somehow, some way, they saw something in Henri they could identify with." Henri dismantled categories that people naturally inhabited in social, political, and religious discourse (such as left and right wing). He made a point of saying he was not interested in issues—for him people and relationships mattered far more.

"He wasn't consciously trying to translate spirituality into psychological terms," Peter Weiskel said. "He was so thoroughly steeped in the Christian spiritual tradition, on the one hand, and so thoroughly honest about his brokenness, on the other. In a way, the brokenness became a vehicle for conveying the message about death and resurrection as a bearer of Jesus. He came to Harvard Divinity School, the epitome of the intellectual life, and resolved to know nothing except Jesus crucified. He got strong responses both ways—for some students, it was a revelation; for others, something they couldn't accept or tolerate."

Henri's passion for peace and social justice molded him into a more political person, whether he liked it or not. At his office in Washington, DC, Jim Wallis, editor-in-chief of *Sojourners* magazine and convener of "The Call to Renewal," recalled how Henri had become involved in Witness for Peace and the Campaign against Nuclear Disarmament. The world of social activism was not a controlled environment, like a liturgy where the priest was celebrating Mass or a spirituality lecture where the speaker was the focus of the hall's attention. Henri entered a stressful, turbulent context and it panicked him at times. For example, when he was speaking on behalf of peace in Nicaragua at a church in Miami, there was a bomb threat, which was frightening. On another occasion, Wallis invited him to speak in Washington, moving from a church service to civil disobedience at the U.S. Capitol. The heady cocktail of surging crowds, media interest, and political pressure was disconcerting and disorienting for a contemplative pastoral minister, but Henri stayed in the thick of it. He did not look or feel at all comfortable, but he insisted on being part of the event.

"He was calling for a contemplative tranquility which was difficult to find in his own heart," said Wallis. "We were close enough for me to see what it means to bring your faith and spirituality to a world that often is not neat, controlled, or has easy answers. Henri struggled. He was not a natural activist by any means. He didn't have the temperament or personality of an activist. In trying to have his faith be active in the world, it was often a stretch for him. But he made the effort time and time again, and, in so doing, I think there was integrity in that search."

Despite being a person who had built a reputation as a spiritual leader and a great man of prayer, Henri was a conflicted soul in many realms, Jim Wallis observed. He could be frenetic in his worrying, anxiety, and nervousness, but he was drawn to an issue because the gospel would compel him. The pace of a speaking tour is challenging for anyone, yet Henri didn't flinch from going around Nicaragua. Witness for Peace was an effort to try to end the killing of innocent civilians by the contras. Supporters would go to civilian areas as a presence of North Americans to create a buffer between the contras and the Nicaraguans who were being attacked. Henri went to Latin America and came back to share what he discovered. "He was right in the middle of an intense political issue and confrontation with the administration of the U.S. government," Wallis recalled. "With strong feelings on both sides, it was not an easy place for a contemplative to be, yet he chose to be there. It was tension-filled, but he got really involved. He wasn't a naturally political person at all. He didn't have much political savvy or strategic sense at all about how to run a campaign or articulate an issue, but he would sense the moral issue, the theological import, the spiritual dimension to these things and that would draw him to it."

So, valiantly, if awkwardly, Henri attempted to make the link and bridge the gap between prayer and peace-making, spirituality and politics, the contemplative life and the activist life. It wasn't always smooth but the fact that he tried was commendable and made him a prophetic figure because there are many who are content to be spiritual leaders, or resources on prayer or spiritual formation, but who hesitate to enter the tempestuous world of social justice and politics. Others without an inner life or spiritual base often become frenzied activists. "If you don't have any roots in prayer and contemplation, you will not last in this very long," said Jim Wallis. "That's why I think the two together are so critical, and Henri, from the contemplative side, tried to do that." But, according to an interview he gave in the early 1980s, Henri was struggling more on the inside rather than with his public work. The rallying speeches to large audiences and the reception he received in different parts of the world created a sense of having arrived. Yet his inner life "was precisely the opposite of that. More and more I felt that if God has anything to say, he doesn't need me. I found myself experiencing two extremes at the same time: high affirmation and great darkness."[8]

Henri's other close association in Washington, DC, was with the Church of the Saviour, where he sometimes preached. He was impressed by its Servant Leadership School, which reflected a more mystical, downwardly mobile approach to ministry. "He brought a marvelous spirit of discipleship and servanthood, a theology that was grounded in the scriptures and the Word but, more than that, lived out with the poor, the dispossessed, and the marginalized," said Don McClanen, who visited him in Peru to learn what ministry among the poor in the United States might mean. "Henri gave such a balanced perspective on poor people and poverty. He was a stabilizing, mature, vital, life-giving servant of Christ in the most wonderful way." Henri was intrigued by the Church's ministry of money, which tried to raise consciousness and bridge the ever-widening gap between the poor and the rich. He agreed that greed, materialism, and consumerism needed to be replaced by grace, joy, and generosity. As a member of a Protestant community, Don paid his Roman Catholic friend the ultimate compliment without appearing sentimental. "The human Jesus as well as the divine Jesus was as much embodied in him as anybody

I have ever known." He also compared him with Augustine, Francis of Assisi, Thomas Merton, and Mother Teresa, people who had come from privileged backgrounds and then had given their lives for others in unusual ways. "I'm not sure you can be a saint without being wounded," Don McClanen said.

4

THE TRUSTING HEART

As to the heart—where else is life if not in the heart?

—Theophan the Recluse

L'Arche came into being in the mid-1960s when many young people, including Jean Vanier, were looking for something to follow other than the path of material success and personal accomplishment. Vanier did not have any reasons as such for starting what became an international network of compassion—it was all based on intuition. He says that he just trusted and loved. Although he couldn't then do anything on a large scale, he felt he could simply help the men to find a decent life and the freedom to be themselves, and so the ark was launched. From the outset, L'Arche was rooted in love with its gospel philosophy that each person, whatever their abilities or disabilities, strengths or weaknesses, was important and sacred. Vanier understood that we discover how we can be healed by those who are the most vulnerable. It was not a matter of going out and ministering to *them* but recognizing that receiving the gift of their presence transforms *us*. This was something Henri Nouwen grew to appreciate as he readjusted to his new milieu during his transitional year at Trosly, north of Paris.

The cofounder of L'Arche, Père Thomas Philippe, probably the most significant companion on Henri Nouwen's mystical journey, was described by some as the St. John of the Cross of his time. After listening to a fervent homily of his on the Assumption of the Virgin Mary and hearing more about the preacher, Henri became aware of the priest's "extraordinary spiritual gifts" and quickly sought him out as a spiritual director. He communicated deeply and convincingly "the mystery of God's presence among us."[1] The experience also brought him closer to the women and men with intellectual disabilities, allowing him to hear, as they did, *with the heart*. Not only did his private meetings with Père Thomas provide profound insights into the mystical journey, they also helped him face his inner demons. In the sessions, Henri was not reticent in sharing his need for affection, which lay at the root of his personal anguish. He was aware that, as he got older, the issue did not diminish. He was worried this thorn in the flesh might choke the development of his spiritual life. The guidance helped him to *think* differently before *feeling* differently. The Dominican priest reminded him that affection was a central concern for many in a culture that had become highly psychologized. Reinforced by a media that seemed to suggest being loved, liked, appreciated, and acknowledged were the most desired prizes of life, people tended to judge themselves in terms of the affection they received or were denied. Lack of affection could lead to acute loneliness, depression, and even suicide. But it was precisely this highly developed psychological consciousness that prevented people from sometimes reaching that place where healing powers were hidden. Henri saw that the priest's greatest gift was "his ability to speak about that place and mobilize its hidden gifts. He calls that place the heart."[2]

Père Thomas saw *the trusting heart* as the most important characteristic of the human person. What made people different from the rest of creation was not their ability to think, reflect, plan, or produce, but their ability to trust, so the heart above all else made people human. This explained why people responded to their surroundings with their hearts, long before their consciences were formed. The conscience gave people a basis for making a moral choice in differentiating between good and evil, but it was less in control of people than the heart, according to Père Thomas, who believed strongly that "the crisis in the Church" was associated with a lack of knowledge of the heart. Ecclesiastical discussions over a range of ethical issues, which had alienated many, focused on the morality of human behavior. But when the moral life received all the attention, people were in peril of overlooking the primacy of the mystical life, which was the life of the heart.

By speaking about the heart as the deepest source of the spiritual life—the life of faith, hope, and love—the Dominican tried to demonstrate to Henri that human affections did not lead us to where our hearts wanted to take us. The heart was more expansive and profound than any affective behavior. It lay before and beyond the distinctions of sorrow and joy, anger and lust, fear and love. It was the place of true belonging where all was one in God, that from which we come and that to which we always yearn to return. Henri was surprised that his simple question about his affections received such a rich spiritual response. "I need to relearn the central place of the mystical experience in human life," he notes.[3]

Henri's transitional year in France led to a position in Canada as pastor at L'Arche Daybreak, Richmond Hill, Ontario. I asked Henri what the move had taught him about God's will in relation to his own desires. "God's will is the way God loves us," he responded.

That's what God's will is about—God's love for us. For a long time in my life, I felt that my own desire, which was to study psychology and later on to become a teacher in psychology, was also my vocation. So, my career and my vocation were not in conflict—I was doing God's will, living according God's love for me, as a university professor. But at one point it felt, suddenly, that there was a conflict between my career and my vocation. My career no longer allowed me to continue my vocation. Then suddenly, I was lost and really didn't know where to go. First, I thought Latin America. Then I went back to university which didn't work. Then I kept praying about it and finally discovered L'Arche. And L'Arche discovered me because people came to see me and invited me. Then I was invited to do something I wasn't at all prepared for. I didn't know anything about mentally handicapped people. I'd never studied them. I wasn't even interested. In a way, it had never been part of my thinking. I was at the university—what they call the place for the best and the brightest—and here I was being called to live with mentally handicapped people. I am totally unpractical in the first place. Everything seemed to be not fitting me, but God called me there. And in this case, God's will was not totally in line with my specific talents.

Henri felt, then, a deep inner sense that he was called, not simply to have a job or to *do* something but to live a specific form of life that was not in tandem with his natural gifts. He came to learn that the very people to whom he had been sent were, in fact, his guides. This was the mystery of the mutuality of true ministry most visible among the poor. He had written about "heart speaking to heart"; now he was experiencing what that meant in a way he had never expected. His deepest wound of needing admiration and fearing rejection was noticeable even during the Masses at L'Arche. He found it difficult to preach to a community that wasn't always attentive to what he was saying or interrupted his passionate homilies with sounds he wasn't familiar with. "I can no longer hide the good news behind my intelligence or rhetorical talents. I am too quickly unmasked!" he once wrote. "When there is something sad to be told there are tears, when there is something joyful to announce there are smiles. When I am boring, I know it directly. When I am inspiring, I know that, too. Those who can speak don't wait until after the service to say it, and those who can walk don't hesitate to walk away or come closer when they feel like it."[4]

The most significant mystical relationship at Daybreak was the one with Adam Arnett, a young man he cared for over the course of fourteen months. During this time, he came to realize how Adam was offering him his body in total vulnerability when he gave himself to him to be undressed, bathed, dressed, fed, and walked from place to place. At the same time, Adam helped Henri become rooted not only in the community but also in his own self and body. Adam kept pulling him back to earth, to the ground of being, to the source of life, educating him about the nature of love. While Adam could not communicate with his caretaker in words, Henri sensed Adam's heart was alive and full of love that could both give and receive. Henri writes as a mystic when he explains,

> As I grew closer to Adam, I came to experience his most beautiful heart as the gateway to his real self, to his person, his soul and his spirit. His heart, so transparent, reflected for me not only his person but also the heart of the universe and, indeed, the heart of God....
>
> I have preached that the divine became manifest in the human so that all things human could become manifestations of the divine. Adam came with others to worship and to hear me preach. He sat in front of me in his chair, and I *saw* the divine significance made visible in him. Adam, I believe, had a heart where the Word of God was dwelling in intimate silence. Adam, during our time together, led me to that intimate indwelling

where the deepest significance of his and my humanity was unfolding.[5]

In his weakness, Adam became a unique instrument of the grace of God in the community, a revelation of Christ even with a radiant inner light "of God."[6] When Henri saw Adam's body lying in his casket after his death in 1996, he was struck by his mystery. He knew Adam was loved by God from all eternity and sent into the world with a unique healing mission, now fulfilled. Adam had become "an image of the living Christ for me just as Jesus, when he lived on the earth, was friend, teacher, and guide for his disciples."[7] Adam Arnett taught him how the body manifested God's grace, and how, in any given moment, one might catch a glimpse of the eternal.

TRULY HUMAN

Many at Daybreak spoke to me of their strong love for their pastor and his deep love for them. The profound fidelity and beauty of Henri's spiritual life spread throughout the community. He welcomed anybody who walked into a room or the chapel with that rare ability to draw them in and love each person individually. House assistant and Anglican priest Wendy Lywood told me,

> The core members just treated him as a normal human being, as Henri. Yes, he was the priest and that was important to people, but more so, he was just Henri. They didn't put him on the pedestal that most people did. By putting him on a pedestal people did him a great dis-service. Our core members treated him as truly human and that's what he needed in order to become who he was. There is an intimacy in that which there isn't when you put someone like Henri on a pedestal. It treats him as somebody other than human

when, in fact, he was very human. When he traveled to give talks, he took community members with him and that was important for him. People might forget what he said but they wouldn't forget that they came together. It gave him some security in knowing that here were people who would be honest with him and treat him just as he was.

Beth Porter explained that, at Daybreak, everyone experienced the suffering of one another, which, in turn, put each person in front of their own suffering. Henri was a priest who had been always "incredibly faithful" during his own pain. The community had rarely experienced someone who had called them to perceive, not only the spiritual meaning of suffering, but also God's love amid that and God's love in one another. This was exemplified most powerfully in the Eucharist, which Henri saw as part of "bodying forth God's presence" before them so, in sharing together as a community, they brought God's presence, love, and justice to one another in that communal moment, something that continued throughout the day. Henri's profound prayer life and his sense of fidelity emerged out of that, along with a capacity to love and be alongside people, as well as to empathize because he was so exceptionally in touch with his own suffering. He was able to be with people in their pain in a space where he offered them faith and hope: the very place of their pain was where God would meet them and help them. It was a message that inspired all who came to hear about it.

He would speak to the seniors' club about grieving and ageing, drawing on his own experience, including the loss of his mother. Once again, words touched people and some listeners would be in tears. It was a gift for being real with people about his own wounds at a level that was helpful to them. He made the suffering he had lived available to others but not in a manner that suggested he was more important than they were. "That was why people loved him so much, especially among the core membership," said Beth. "They loved someone who was able himself to be vulnerable, and people could make themselves vulnerable in front of him. There was such a bond. He had great compassion for people who were hurting. There were many in the community whom he hugged and let them cry against him."

This natural compassion flowed on one memorable occasion when Henri took part in a discussion with a rabbi and an imam. The room was packed—with students, older people, and many from the Daybreak community. During questions, an elderly woman in the front row, in a voice that was breaking, asked how Christians could interpret a particular aspect of Holy Scripture in an anti-Semitic way; she then talked about how she had been in a concentration camp where her parents had died. The room was silent. As she began to speak, Henri moved around the desk and sat on the edge. Then, as he went to respond to her, he crouched down in front of her, made eye contact and spoke directly to her. He acknowledged that her concerns were very important, especially for the Church. Then, as the Christian representative, he went on to apologize on behalf of the Church for what she had suffered, even though the point she had raised about the scriptures had been a tough question. "He validated her at every level," Beth recalled. "This was a woman who could hardly get her question out, and was in tears as she was asking it. It was a very prophetic moment."

Henri's ministry at L'Arche led him to reflect theologically on the nature of Christian leadership. In his book *In the Name of Jesus*, he says that for Christian leadership to be fruitful, it needs to move from the moral to the mystical. Henri concludes that the only necessary focus for the spiritual leader of the future is the contemplative discipline of dwelling in the presence of the One who keeps asking (like Jesus to Peter), "Do you love me? Do you love me? Do you love me?" Did this possibly remind him of his questions from the playpen? Through contemplative prayer, says Henri, ministers can prevent themselves from being overwhelmed by urgent issues "and from becoming strangers to our own and God's heart." It is inadequate for priests and ministers to be solely moral people, however important that might be. The heart of Christian leadership is about whether or not they are truly men and women of God—"with an ardent desire to dwell in God's presence, to listen to God's voice, to look at God's beauty, to touch God's incarnate Word, and to taste fully God's infinite goodness."[8] Henri reminds readers that the original meaning of *theology* is "union with God in prayer" but points out that it has become one academic discipline among many, and even theologians find it difficult to pray. He contends therefore that it is of vital importance to reclaim the mystical aspect of theology so that every word spoken, every piece of advice given, and every strategy can emerge from a heart that knows God intimately.

In the brokenness of the core members, Henri discovered a hidden blessing—a power of God's presence. God was saying good things (blessing) in the very places where people were weak. That was where the healing power of God could become manifest. Day by day, he was living among people who could not talk or walk but who radiated God's healing power through their vulnerability. His empowerment did not come from his being known as a spiritual leader but from living among the poor who, because they did not have to prove anything, could live out the truth of who they were. The core members taught Henri how to communicate more effectively and, in the process, how to know them better.

While Henri could speak eloquently about community, he did not manage to live it quite so gracefully. At Daybreak, he continued to travel, not only from his new base, but across it—as fast as he could in his small blue Honda. Kathy Christie, who was Henri's secretary for four-and-a-half years, never forgot the day she came for her second interview, leaving her young daughter, Stacey, in the car. After their chat, Henri rushed out to his Honda, swept Stacey out of Kathy's car and into his back seat, then drove crazily around the property showing them various aspects as fast as he could. "It was just like a whirlwind," Kathy said. "I think we saw all of Daybreak in about 15 minutes. But in that, he was so embracing and accepting of us."

After she got the job, the pair would start at 8:00 a.m., work intensely for half an hour, then Henri would literally run off to Mass. Worshipers quietly praying in the chapel grew accustomed to hearing the outside door banging, the inside door being flung open, and Henri tearing through, sometimes crashing into furniture, and genuflecting on the run. He had it off pat, making a little dip with his knees as he went by the tabernacle, then disappearing into the sacristy before reemerging seconds later wearing his alb and stole. Then he would sit there and sing a Taizé chant like *Ubi caritas et amor, Deus ibi est* (Where charity and love are, God is there). In some ways, the community observed, Henri was "so deeply there," but in other ways, he was "just so gone," a delightful combination of humanity.

Henri would be back in the office at nine, spending the rest of the morning with Kathy Christie on manuscripts and correspondence. He received between sixty and seventy letters every week and insisted on responding to everything personally, sending complimentary books if he didn't reply by letter. He had "tons and tons" of invitations from all over the world, which he found hard to decline. "When Henri came into the office, he filled the room with his energy," said Kathy who, in working so closely with the author, saw his paradoxes at first hand:

> In some ways, he could be the most insecure individual you could ever meet, and then in the next moment he was the most secure individual that you could meet in terms of his spirituality. When someone with a problem came to see Henri, the focus was total. He had this ability to zero in on whatever was bothering the person, this gift of totally being there with them. So,

while in his personal life the insecurities were there, in his spiritual life, in his life where he gave to other people, he was totally secure. When you listened to him preach, he was so sure in his faith. He absolutely lived it. He had doubts and conflicts but not when it came to that part of his life.

Henri found it virtually impossible to write his books at Daybreak. As much as he desired space, he was also keen to be part of everything. People also wanted to talk to him, be counseled, or receive spiritual accompaniment. So, Henri would go to friends' houses in Ontario or Europe, but even then, he kept in touch almost daily. He was obsessive about his work at L'Arche. The office grounded him at Daybreak, and he was keen to know that this connection remained solid while he was away. Kathy Christie never experienced him as a relaxed person except when he was at Freiburg in Germany writing *Our Greatest Gift: A Meditation on Caring and Dying*.[9] He stayed in an apartment at his German editor's house and would fax pages over for her to type up. "There was a peacefulness in his writing that book. Once he got going, it just flowed. He seemed to find there a quiet space in himself as well as in the environment. He wasn't so much frantically calling and worrying about what was going on in the community. From a distance, I really felt he was calm at that time."

From his earliest times at L'Arche, Henri's movements outside the community, responding to so many demands on his time, became the subject of concern. How could he be a faithful pastor there if he were being drawn in so many directions? Initially, leaders told Henri that they thought he was spending too much time away. Taking the feedback seriously, he invited a circle of people to help him sift his invitations and prioritize. Over 95 percent of them were subsequently declined. Nonetheless, despite his schedule, outer demands, and book deadlines, Henri was available to people in an extraordinary way. To help him relax, he was persuaded to join a men's group that met regularly. On one occasion, the members invited him on a canoe expedition. In characteristic style, Henri turned up in a trench coat and a suitcase on wheels that he had to drag unceremoniously between lakes. Henri walked off way ahead of everyone else, then turned and asked, "Where are we going?" "Gate 4," came the reply. But Henri nevertheless proved to be a delightful, engaging companion, celebrating Mass every day in the woods and sharing his life through many conversations.

As he began to grow older, his energy became more limited than it had been, and, wisely, he sensed that his pastoral time might be better used by informing others how to carry on his work rather than doing everything himself. Quite consciously, he took upon himself the responsibility of developing a pastoral team that enabled the community to flourish. The community also accepted that it would, in fact, be dangerous for it to become too dependent on Henri or any other individual in terms of its pastoral life. They also acknowledged that Henri Nouwen was larger than Daybreak or L'Arche itself—and he couldn't be possessed or controlled. They provided a home for him, a community to hang on to him, but recognized that he needed to be made available for many other people and many other ministries to which he had dedicated his life.

At L'Arche, they told me, Henri "walked around with his depth."

5

WOUND AND BLESSING

Our wounds are ultimately our greatest source of blessing because they become one with the wounds of our humble God.

—Maggie Ross, Christian solitary

It has been well documented that Henri was a complex figure, but it is not possible to understand his psychology without considering his sexual identity. His loneliness may have had many sources, but the way he writes about it is analogous to the gay person's experience, as many readers discerned. Every one of us is a sexual being, and the subject should always be discussable without embarrassment. But when it comes to a celibate priest and his sexuality, there are always some people who think the blinds should stay firmly closed. I am reminded, however, of an American nun who told me that suggestions she did not have sexual feelings were "damnable," and of the Benedictine monk who said, "I shall be a sexual being until my last breath." Henri, who said he knew his orientation at the age of six, claimed his sexuality was not the most interesting dimension of his personality, even though he was always aware of its power. His struggles as a celibate priest have been publicly known for two decades, yet even now there is a tendency at times to dehumanize him by pretending that he was not a sexual being, which is clearly ridiculous because he both wrote and spoke about his sexual feelings.

Unfortunately, it is difficult for any author to write about the subject positively, or helpfully for others, without facing accusations of being polemical. No one knew this more than Henri. This was why he was cautious about "'coming out" himself. He felt some readers might think he had an agenda and would reject him as an author, someone writing from the point of his sexuality rather than his spirituality. It is important to remember as well, though, that Henri's struggles as a gay man, particularly in the realm of devastating loneliness, undoubtedly influenced and flowered into his brilliant spiritual writing. Henri's fears about being attacked by the religious right if he disclosed his sexuality were not, however, unfounded: since his death, there have been backlashes on the internet, while one alarmed Catholic priest in the Diocese of Phoenix banned all Henri's publications from his bookstore. Such irrational fear was one reason why Henri was keen to write about sexuality from a contemplative perspective. When we met, four years before he died, he told me,

> I haven't found yet the best ways to write about sexuality because I still have the feeling that in order to write well about sexuality you have to speak about it from the place of mysticism and not just from the place of morality. When you speak about morality, we deal with questions about what you're allowed to do and what you're not allowed to do, what's good and what's not so good, and all that. I do think there are a lot of discussions on that level and I don't feel any need to join in these discussions, not that they are useless—that's not my vocation. But I have a very strong feeling that

there's something to be said about sexuality, and about intimacy and sexuality, which has to come from a place of communion. You see, the whole question of sexuality is also a question of communion—intercourse, people talk about. Communion, intimacy; it involves our bodies as well as our minds and our hearts. But if we talk about sexuality from the place of communion, we first of all to have to speak well about the depths of what communion is about—communion as that which our heart most desires and, from that place, we might start talking about sexuality and sexual life. Every human being lives a sexual life, whether you're celibate or married or whatever. Sexual life is life. That sexual life has to be lived as a life that deepens the communion with God and with our fellow human beings. And if it doesn't, then it can be very harmful. I haven't found the right language for it yet and hope I will one day.

Some people, especially isolated priests who are gay, regret that the linguistic breakthrough never happened, because they believe Henri's words could have given them encouragement and spiritual guidance. He, of all people, knew what it was like to be a priest who was gay. Here was a world-class writer, as close to their experience as anyone could be, who could really have made a difference to their lives. Furthermore, there are many in the gay community who wish Henri had been more open about himself during his lifetime. A gay priest in America told me, "I think part of the tragedy for Henri and for others is that many readers knew he was gay. His gamble not to mention it makes his work, however genius, somewhat tainted with fear and lacking in integrity. It's a risk he took but I believe it was part of the sad 'don't ask, don't tell' mentality. This allows gay priest writers to have acceptance and influence in straight society rather than 'taking up the cross' and perhaps, with more honesty, helping the lost souls who really need hope—instead of writing for the privileged who sometimes regard spirituality as a beautiful enhancement of their lives."

While this may well be a plausible perspective, spiritual authors in the national or international spotlight know how hard it is to write as they would wish about homosexuality, especially if they happen to be Roman Catholic priests. In fact, Henri, noted for being an open book, was constantly troubled by the fact that he did not feel he could be more frank about this dimension of his life about which he was well informed. For many years, he read voraciously on the subject, buying hundreds of books and journals to deepen his knowledge. It was not a fleeting interest but an academic and personal study of a topic that preoccupied him over the course of his life.

Although Henri had realized his orientation as a child, homosexuality was never discussed in the home, like most other households at the time, while the Roman Catholic Church regarded the state as a mental illness and any practice of it a sin. Yet again, Henri had grown up feeling estranged and alienated. While he was at Yale in the 1970s, however, he bravely composed a brilliant article on the subject, which has not been widely read to this day. It would greatly help the Church to understand the psychological dynamics of being gay, something it tends to overlook. The subject must have been simmering inside Henri for a long time, especially through the days of his psychological formation, and clearly, he felt a need to express what he felt about it in writing. The opportunity came when he was asked to write a chapter, "The Self-Availability of the Homosexual," for the book *Is Gay Good?*, crafted from the thinking of the Dutch psychiatrist W. G. Sengers.[1] The chapter reasons that sexual feelings for homosexual people are just as real, personal, and intimate as for heterosexuals; therefore, suggesting they can change their feelings is a direct offense to "their most precious selves." The underlying issue for homosexuals is this: How can they relate meaningfully to their own sexual feelings in a culture where such feelings are already judged and evaluated before they can even begin to make them their own? Homophobia makes it difficult for them to come to terms with their sexuality and relate to their feelings realistically. For human beings of any sexuality to relate meaningfully to their own selves, they must be *available* to themselves, Henri argues. This isn't easy for homosexuals because they're easily conditioned by who they think they already are because of what other people have said about them over the course of their lives. They might fundamentally judge themselves as victims of discrimination or bullying, members of a persecuted minority, those who don't really belong, or people who have experienced shame and rejection. These negative images are then internalized, distorting their self-image and damaging their self-confidence. In that process, feelings get suppressed or repressed. Much suffering is the result of detachment from feelings that were never made available.

So, in any culture hostile to homosexuality, Henri says, it's understandable that a person who experiences homosexual feelings might be inclined to disown themselves from those feelings and put them on the periphery of their experience. The idea of being a homosexual is so loaded with fear that many people prefer to resist their true feelings rather than relate to them realistically *as their own*. The erotic feelings a person might have toward someone of the same sex should only be experienced as positive. Love is about beauty and freedom, so the strong attraction between two people of the same sex should be something valuable and enriching. In reality, however, this is not always the case. The growing awareness of erotic feelings toward people of the same sex creates feelings of shame, low self-esteem, and a fear of difference and potential rejection. Feelings that are in themselves positive tend to be condemned by those who experience them. What is actually good is filtered as bad, while what is positive is interpreted as negative because people adapt their feelings, not to their own perceptions, but to what others say about them. The resistance or denial of these feelings can create massive psychological issues.

Henri outlines the two levels of resistance—repression and suppression. Homosexuals who repress their sexuality completely deny their inclinations to others but primarily to themselves. This cuts them off from their own most personal, intimate, and creative feelings, forcing them to evacuate to the safe place of cerebral life. "If we do this," Henri writes, "we become rigid, impersonal, distant and controlling. This does great harm to the personality, creating emotional poverty." Sliding into the second level of resistance, suppression, homosexual people know and understand their feelings but are careful not to communicate them to anyone else because they are tortured by the fear that other people might get to know about them. They always *pretend* to be heterosexual and are never in situations where they can be themselves and express their true feelings. They become so tormented by the fear of becoming known as a homosexual that their sexual feelings constantly preoccupy them and sexualize their total existence. Every situation becomes open to danger, and they are constantly on their guard to prevent anyone from discovering their sexuality. It is impossible for the sexual life of a suppressed person to form a unity with the rest of their personality. This distorts social reality. Henri stresses that sexual feelings touch the core of the internal lives of homosexuals. If they pretend not to have those feelings, it is "like living without a heart." When they overcome their resistance, however, they can start to make their sexual feelings *available to themselves* and give them a place at the center of their own lives. If they do this, they will begin to relate to their feelings realistically.

Christian morality has never advocated the denial of feelings, only a responsible way of relating to them, Henri explains. We act morally only when we are able to face the reality of our lives and make our decisions from there. Feelings are never moral or immoral in themselves—only the way we relate to them. He says that if a person feels a strong erotic love for someone of the same sex, they experience "a deep human feeling" that tells them very much about themselves. Yet if they think, talk, or act as if this feeling isn't there at all, they mutilate their emotional life and are in danger of psychological paralysis. But if homosexuals make their real feelings *available to themselves* and recognize them as their *own* feelings, then they can make a moral decision about the way they want to live their lives. This could include developing a deep relationship, channeling their emotional energy into a social concern, making the feelings part of a contemplative life, or opting to live a celibate existence, but the feelings need to be owned first, liberated from the fear of prejudice or rejection, and integrated into the total personality. "The gospel makes it overwhelmingly clear that Christ came to reveal the real human condition and to challenge people to face it without fear. Christ does not judge feelings or emotions. He only asks people not to deny or distort them but instead to make them available for God's love."[2]

When I discussed the article with a retreat group, an Irish Catholic gay man disclosed that he would have been spared much psychological suffering in his life had he known of its existence. "When I was nineteen, I was told by a counselor, who happened to be a priest, that the feelings I was experiencing were a homosexual phase," Alan told us. "I believed him. Why wouldn't I? He said I ought to go out to discos at weekends and meet women, like everyone else. I did, but my homosexual feelings didn't go away. I didn't know I was gay until I finally had the courage to come out to myself when I was twenty-four. If I had read healthy, affirming articles like Henri Nouwen's, I would have begun the slow process of acceptance quicker.

"I struggled for many years to integrate my sexuality with my spirituality. I kept separating them rather than realizing that they were one. I stopped going to Mass and Church for a while but went back, not only out of cultural, family, and community tradition, but also because I felt somehow that I was loved by and welcomed by God. I just wish I had read Henri's article in my teenage years. It could have started me on the road to self-acceptance much sooner. The message which struck a particular chord with me was that it was all right to have homosexual feelings and to feel sexually attracted to someone of the same sex. It was healthy, and it was okay being me. God wants us to be ourselves. He does not want to deny or suppress our true feelings and emotions."

A few weeks later, when I gave a presentation on Nouwen and Pastoral Care at a Roman Catholic parish in Kent, England, I saw no reason to allude to Henri's sexuality. However, the subject arose during question time, and it was plain that parishioners were eager to discuss the issue openly, not having many other opportunities. One of those present was a seventy-seven-year-old retired accountant, Romilly Turton, who said he had always found Henri Nouwen's writing a deep source of meditative prayer and reflection. "The way in which he tackles brokenness in our lives, and shows how the redemptive love of Christ embraces the *totality* of who we are, is strikingly different from other religious writers," he pointed out. Later, when Romilly read "The Self-Availability of the Homosexual," he found himself agreeing entirely with the Nouwen approach. "Unfortunately, I grew up a bigot and it took me many years to understand the predicament of homosexuals," he told me. "When Nouwen wrote that piece, the American Psychiatric Association still classified homosexuality as a sociopathic personality disturbance. It was not until 1973 that it was dropped as a diagnostic category. Yet people still speak of 'healing homosexuality' and 'reparative therapy,' which is so sad. Today, it is easy to overlook just how courageous it was of Nouwen as a Roman Catholic priest to write so enlighteningly on a subject that was normally avoided altogether and considered far too controversial to tackle sensitively."

Henri distributed copies of the "The Self-Availability of the Homosexual" to his students at Yale. It cannot be overemphasized how difficult it was for him, as a Roman Catholic priest, to speak any more openly about sexuality at that time. One gay priest in Ireland told me that he fully understood Henri's predicament. He explained how, in leading any community in prayer, a priest represented gospel values or what it was to be a good person. This led to a keen sense of the gap between what the priest proclaimed and who he truly was. In a real sense, a priest was always a sinner and could never be fully what he proclaimed. Since its early days, the Church had been clear that the grace given through the liturgy was offered by Christ, irrespective of the celebrant's virtue or lack of it. As a more general phenomenon, clericalism had placed high value on the explicit visibility of the priest as a witness to the gospel. The common perception, traceable to the scriptures, was that the priest should be a model of virtue. For the priest, then, who was gay, to the extent that he was homophobic about his own gayness, he was bound to experience "a great deal of dissonance" between his public "virtuous" persona and who he was in himself. Certainly, an intrinsic element in coping with dissonance is "coming out" or allowing one's homosexuality to become self-available, as Henri had written. But the priest believed that this self-availability could only happen through coming out in some key interpersonal contexts of one's life.

The priest told me, "We cannot give it to ourselves by prayer, reflection, reading, writing, or willpower. Nouwen illustrates this so well. After all, he knew his sexual orientation as a boy but only began to come out to others—and to himself—later as a mature man, and then never did so fully." The priest's point was that it is only by sharing their sexuality with a friend, spiritual director, sibling, or parent that gay people can really know themselves to be acceptable "in their gayness." He went on to explain that, in terms of a priest, it was precisely his public liturgical role that made the essential coming-out process such a fearful step to make. To the extent that congregations, communities, fellow clergy, or bishops were themselves homophobic, priests who came out raised fears of scandal and even prejudice over their opportunities to serve. The priest went on to say, "One is exposed—stretched between dissonance and disaster. These, perhaps, were the stakes Henri

Nouwen had lived at a degree of extreme visibility. It all points to the need for more honesty and openness which could normalize the dissonance and not dramatize it in unhealthy and unnatural ways. That was Nouwen's salvation in the dark hours."

But in January 1976, while associate professor of pastoral theology at Yale, Henri was prepared to put his head above the parapet in defense of Ensign Vernon E. Berg III, who was facing dismissal from the U.S. Navy for being homosexual in a married relationship. Writing to "The Officers of the Court Martial" in Norfolk, Virginia, on Yale Divinity School notepaper, Henri says the case has been brought to his attention and that he has been asked to make a statement in Berg's defense. "I am happy to do so," he states, adding,

> As a Catholic priest I am very much aware of the complex issues around the morality of overt homosexual behavior, and I realize that the question, if a homosexual lifestyle is a viable option for a Christian, is difficult to answer. I am, nonetheless, deeply concerned that these issues and questions should be carefully separated from the question of whether homosexuality makes someone less competent to be a Naval officer.
>
> As soon as the question of morality is linked with the question of competence in a certain field of work, there is indeed an imminent danger of discrimination which can lead easily to serious harm to the principles of freedom and equality.
>
> In defense of Ensign Berg, I would like to state that I do not believe that sexual preference as such affects competence in the field and therefore hope that Ensign Berg can be considered as a fully qualified Naval officer independent of his sexual preference.

Six months later, Berg was dismissed and later took out a lawsuit against the Navy, which is credited with ending the practice of giving homosexuals less than honorable discharges. Henri was certainly not a lone theological or academic voice offering support for Berg at the time, but he may not have realized his letter would be included as a selected affidavit in a book about the case, published two years later.[3] (Among the other statements is a letter from John Boswell, who was assistant professor of history at Yale during Henri's tenure. He would later write the award-winning *Christianity, Social Tolerance, and Homosexuality.*[4])

ECCLESIA SPIRITUALIS

As Henri's popularity as a spiritual author blossomed in the 1970s and '80s, he played it safe by giving sexuality a wide berth. This is probably because he was starting to write more personally and knew that, if he made too many references to the subject in his books, suspicious readers might alert the Catholic authorities who, in turn, would inform Rome. In this regard, Henri was always a highly sensitive priest not only in view of persisting homophobia in society at large, but also, of course, because of his own Church's position, though, interestingly, the Dutch Catechism considered homosexuality "morally neutral," a statement the Vatican did not oppose.[5] As he was an author who liked to share some of his struggles in print, Henri Nouwen knew he had to be careful when it came to sexuality. Even so, his writings still became the main means of processing what he was going through psychologically—without being specific in the case of his orientation. Nonetheless, gay and lesbian readers were not slow in noticing that his articulation of loneliness in *Reaching Out* mirrored their own experience with overwhelming accuracy. For one canon in the Church of England, who could not accept his gay sexuality, the book offered him mysterious solace and encouragement when he had most needed it, bringing meaning into a life of confusion and speaking to a heart in bewilderment. In the book, Henri writes about the spiritual life as being a constantly flowing movement between polarities: between the poles of loneliness and solitude (the relationship to oneself), hostility and hospitality (the relationship to others), and between illusion and prayer (the relationship with God). Like Henri, the canon experienced his own life as a continual state of movement and change. He desired intimacy yet at the same time feared it. He sought aloneness but craved companionship. "I was struggling with depression, the church's view on homosexuality, and a strong desire to be still and alone with God," he said. "Henri Nouwen's writing resonated with profound reality and integrity. Here was a man who articulated my struggles with clarity, gentleness, and empathy. These polarities had sometimes torn away at me so negatively that I wondered who I was. But Henri Nouwen reminded me that I could not bypass them."

It was none other than Carl Jung who observed that homosexual people were often endowed with an abundance of religious feelings, which made them responsive to revelation. He said they also had a natural propensity toward the intuitive, helping them to bring about the *ecclesia spiritualis*. John McNeill, a Catholic priest and writer on homosexuality, told me that Henri Nouwen's writings bore all the hallmarks of Jung's perceptions, such as sensitivity, beauty, compassion, a sense of history, and receptivity. He said he had strongly identified with Henri on the spiritual level because he was in touch with the feminine in himself, which was why gay people found an affinity in his writings: "Nouwen had an extraordinary share in the suffering of loneliness and depression, his own crucifixion, his own dark night of the soul. This had something to do with his gayness. Our greatest wound is always interiorized self-rejection and fear that we are not loved by God. Nouwen's spirituality spoke in a special way to gay experience. But it also has a universal resonance for all who search for an intimate relationship of love with God."

McNeill cautioned, however, against any overanalysis of Henri Nouwen's sexuality. He felt no person had the right to ask whether he should have come out or to suggest he would have been happier if he had left the priesthood. Although McNeill had no personal knowledge of Henri's life, he told me that he believed Henri's special relationship with God had been on a par with St. John of the Cross in terms of its intensity. He sensed God had asked special sacrifices of Henri to cultivate that intense personal relationship with him. "I accept with St. Augustine the belief that 'God made us for God's self and our hearts will not rest until they rest in God.' We who are gay need to have a direct and personal experience of God's love, an experience that frees us from all external voices. I know in my own case that Nouwen's writings showed me the way to that personal experience."

Although Henri was careful about his public endorsement of gay issues, I discovered that, back in the early 1980s, he quietly gave his blessing to the work of the New Ways Ministry, which was developing its work for lesbian and gay people in the Church. Founded by Sister Jeannine Gramick and Father Robert Nugent, the ministry attempted to build bridges between the gay and lesbian community and the Catholic Church. While the ministry was generally accepted by rank-and-file Catholics, the cofounders were investigated and censured by the Vatican. For reasons of conscience, Sister Jeannine refused to be silenced and continues in the ministry to this day.

"Father Nugent and I met Henri Nouwen at a reception at the Canadian embassy in Washington, DC," she told me. "We spoke with him afterwards and he knew of us, even though our ministry had only just begun. He did not speak of his own struggles but actually congratulated us and wished us well because he felt it was a very important ministry. I think it did a lot, in particular, for Father Robert who was a great admirer of Henri Nouwen. I knew of Henri Nouwen, but it was much more of an encouragement for Bob to feel that a great spiritual writer would commend us and encourage us to continue what we were doing. It meant a lot to him. Nouwen was very gracious, a very gentle man. To me he exuded kindness and lovingness, and also an understanding of human nature. That's what he projected to me."

Sister Jeannine said it was crucial that the stories of well-known gay Catholics, like Henri Nouwen, were known after their deaths because confused young people needed role models. "I became a woman religious because I was very impressed by the sisters who taught me," she explained. "When you're young, you look up to people and admire them. If a child is growing up and discovering their same-sex orientation, and the only image they have is that being gay is not good or something to be ashamed of, what does that do to that child's sense of self-esteem? It's not just children: we all need people that we can relate to and so that's why it's so important to know there are lesbian and gay people in all professions including religious life and the priesthood." She acknowledged the difficulties involved in revealing a famous spiritual person's sexuality after their death but said there were broader implications to bear in mind. Individuals did not only belong to their own biological or religious family; they might have an extensive ministry to people across the world, as Henri did. Sister Jeannine said she understood how famous people could become worried by the consequences and dangers of coming out. "You don't want to disappoint or give people the wrong impression, and you don't want people to misinterpret. Yet, I guess we have to trust in God."

Henri had been right in trying to understand sexuality from a mystical perspective. "Unfortunately, we have this idea of equating sexuality with sex," she told me. "Sexuality is part of the total personality. We are all sexual beings, so we can't separate the person from their sexuality—and sexuality gives life and energy to an individual. To see sexuality as mystical is the correct approach. It's taking sexuality out of the category of rules and regulations, and considering sexuality as a life force. In sharing your sexuality, you are sharing your life force. There are, of course, degrees of sharing your sexuality. I think you even share it if you just touch someone. We don't think of touch as a sexual expression, but it is. I would love to have seen Nouwen develop the mystical dimension to sexuality more fully. Sexuality and spirituality are intertwined."

The common anxiety among gay and lesbian people was the fear of not being loved, she said. Everyone had implanted in their hearts the desire to be loved, so there was always the fear that if a mother, father, or coworker discovered a person's gay sexuality, they would not be liked or loved anymore. "They think they'll be rejected," Sister Jeannine continued. "There are varying degrees but, at the root of it, I think, is the ultimate fear of rejection, of not being loved. I think what gave Henri Nouwen the insight into that fear of not being loved was the fear of being known as gay. From my experience of speaking to people and of myself, it's not unusual for children to know their sexuality. We can have a sexual awakening when we're young. There is some consciousness then of sexual differences, even though we might not have the terminology, so it would not have been unusual that Nouwen would have been aware of his sexuality as a boy."

It took a long time for Henri to accept that spirituality and sexuality were not enemies, but friends grafted from the same source, *eros* (desire), even though he had long known that the words *wound* and *blessing* share the same linguistic root. A wound, then, carries within it the power to bless. *Blessure* in French means "wound." If you trace the word *blessing* to Old English via prehistoric Germanic, you find it closely related to *bleed* and *blood*. The word *blessing* comes from Old English: *bletsian, bledsian, bloedsian*. It means "to sanctify or consecrate with blood." Literally *to bless*, then, means "to mark with blood." Henri came to believe that gay and lesbian people, shouldering their own wounds of rejection and hurt, were a blessing to the Church. He even said gay men and women had a special vocation in the Christian community. Gay friends entering into a civil partnership in Canada were reminded of their "holy commitment," while in Ireland he met a Catholic woman who, in some desperation, confided to him that she was a lesbian. She said that, with love and compassion in his eyes, Henri told her that her sexual orientation was a "blessing from God," and from then on, her life changed remarkably.

Several people told me how, in the last few years of his life, Henri became much more comfortable with his sexuality and began to embrace his gay self—or, to use his own words, to become "available to himself." If you read the journal of his final year, *Sabbatical Journey*, it is not difficult to discern that, at times, he is in two minds about his future but is careful not to be too specific. There has been speculation by some friends that Henri was on the brink of leaving the priesthood, but this has been firmly denied by others. Nonetheless, although Henri became more at ease with his sexual orientation in his later years, ultimately it does not appear to have brought him inner peace, as this extract from a letter to a friend in July 1996 (two months before his death) discloses:

> My sexuality will remain a great source of suffering to me until I die. I don't think there is any "solution." The pain is truly "mine" and I have to own it. Any "relational solution" will be a disaster. I feel deeply called by God to live my vows well even when it means a lot of pain. But I trust that the pain will be fruitful.[6]

Brad Colby, who worked at L'Arche with Henri, told me, "He shared his utter anguish about sexuality—on his level of understanding sexuality as mystical, pointing to full unity with the God head, whereas previously it had been something to be overcome in order to achieve mystical union. I think AIDS broke him open in that. He was a mystic who happened to be a priest who happened to be gay."

Jan ter Laak, who, like Henri, knew the pains of being both a priest and a gay man, felt that if Henri had lived longer, he would have written about his sexual orientation. "His plan was to do this," he said. "In all his books, he is telling about his struggles and he wanted to tell this one. You can't understand him without his orientation. For him, to be celibate was important. But he also had strong feelings in friendship, and, for him, this was a struggle to the end."

Jan discovered this in his conversations with Henri after they renewed their friendship in 1989. That day, Jan told him he was gay. Later, Henri phoned him and said he wanted to speak with him. He seemed glad to have discovered a priest and a friend in the Netherlands who was open about his sexuality, though Jan had to leave the priesthood. Some years later, Henri and Jan visited a man dying from AIDS in a Toronto hospital. Jan was also at his side when Henri addressed the National Catholic AIDS Network in Chicago, telling delegates,

> You belong to the people who went before you. You can talk about the saints like St. Francis or Benedict or Ignatius and that is important, but because you have thousands of people who went before you, they are a new family. You have to hold onto them. You have to embrace them as saints. Yes, those who were born and died long ago struggled like me and were anguished like me. They had their sexual struggles as I have, and they were lonely and depressed and confused. They went through the Black Plague. They are a part of my human family.[7]

While friends and readers continue to sympathize with Henri Nouwen's struggles over his sexuality, and have been genuinely moved by his predicament, perhaps only a gay man can *truly* understand what he went through—and what it cost him.

6

NOCHE OSCURA

On the road to union with God the night of faith shall guide me.

—John of the Cross

From the earliest years of the Christian mystical tradition, darkness has been a recurring pattern, influenced by the Book of Exodus where Moses drew near to "the thick darkness where God was" (Exod 20:21). In the *Mystical Theology* of Pseudo-Dionysius, the imagery represents the incomprehensibility of God. Writers such as Meister Eckhart, Johannes Tauler, and Jan van Ruusbroec, as well as the author of *The Cloud of Unknowing*, develop this thinking in their own ways. It was, however, St. John of the Cross, writing in sixteenth-century Spain, who became most noted for this symbolism. For him, the human pilgrimage to God is night— night's purification of attachments, night as a journey of faith, and night as the encounter with the God of mystery. His famous poem "The Dark Night" (*Noche Oscura*) reflects on union with God in love, along with the purification of the senses and the spirit, and the blessings of spiritual enlightenment. "The dark night of the soul" has sometimes been misappropriated, signifying any traumatic spiritual or psychological experience, whereas for John of the Cross, the dark night is specifically God's work, specifically preparing the soul for union with God in love. Night is always for the sake of light and love. In the nineteenth century, St. Thérèse of Lisieux, writing in her own distinct idiom, describes her trial of faith as a night that lasted nearly two years. It was only natural that Henri Nouwen was drawn to Thérèse's writings as well as those of St. John of the Cross.

It was while he was in France preparing for his new future at L'Arche that Henri developed a deep and nurturing platonic friendship with a younger, heterosexual man, Nathan Ball, who came with him to work as a part-time assistant in the Richmond Hill community while studying theology in Toronto. In Henri's mind, the friendship was as significant as his new vocation as a pastor to the developmentally disabled, so when he arrived at Daybreak in August 1986, with a whole new life unfolding before him, he was, unsurprisingly, in a buoyant mood. This is borne out by an unpublished letter, written by Henri on Daybreak notepaper and posted to Michael Harank, of the Catholic Worker movement, who was Henri's first administrative assistant at Harvard Divinity School:

27 August '86

Dear Michael,

Thanks, thanks, thanks for your beautiful letter, so full of your affection and love. It was so good to be with you and share with you my struggles and my joys. It feels very very good to be known and loved by you. I am so glad we found that place where we can be vulnerable together and feel together the strength of God's love.

It is a real joy to know that you are there, know me, love me and hold me close in your prayers. You are very close to me and I want you to claim me as a friend who loves you deeply and wants to give you all you ask for. God has been very good to bring us closer to each other.

The trip went very well. It was a time of joy, friendship, celebration and good work. After all was set up I flew to Calgary to spend a week with Nathan at his parents' retreat center.

It was a glorious week. Much time to sleep, eat, pray and solidify our friendship. The only setback: I totalled my car the day after I bought it (21 km on the odometer). Happily no personal accidents. I must have some special guardian angels!

Please keep in touch. Your letters bring me joy and peace. Never forget what a wonderful gifted man you are, deeply loved by God and those who have the privilege to truly know you.

With lots of love

Henri

Michael Harank remembered how the letter had brought tears of joy to his eyes because it had expressed Henri's genuine feelings about their own developing friendship. It also revealed Henri's excitement over finally arriving at L'Arche in Richmond Hill, where he had been welcomed with open arms. On his way to Richmond Hill, Henri had, in fact, stopped by briefly at the Noonday Catholic Worker farm where Michael was living at the time. There he had articulated his only-too-natural fears, anxieties, and concerns about taking a new step on his spiritual pilgrimage, but he was thrilled about it as well. "We had shared deeply from the well of our personal stories and struggles, and his words truly touched my heart when he wrote," Michael said. "I, too, had been struggling with the issues of being gay, and we talked about the struggles which we shared. His encouragement was truly helpful in my own journey to freedom." When Henri sought Michael's view on the invitation to join Daybreak, Michael asked him whether he wanted to save his soul, telling him, "The different abled and disabled people will teach you to move into the deepest unexplored regions of your humanity, especially the places of silence where there are no words. You will have to learn a whole other language, the language of the heart. Some of their hearts have been broken and wounded so many times that they themselves have frequently lost the language of expression. They will become *your* teachers after all your years of teaching."

As Henri had approached the new life in community, he had come to think about his friendship with Nathan as the safe place amid all the transitions, but he could sometimes prove overpowering in friendships, as Nathan—and others—discovered. By Henri's own admission, his dependence on Nathan prevented him from making the community itself the focus of his life. Colleagues told me that it was more than infatuation on his part. Henri had fallen in love and felt loved, but it was not emotionally reciprocal. Feeling loved is not the same as being loved. When the expectations Henri put on the friendship resulted in its being "interrupted," as the situation has been euphemistically described, Nathan was forced to retreat and Henri found his idyllic new world falling apart as he faced the tragic consequences of unrequited love. Most of Henri's books up until that point had contained some reference or other about how we "crave for someone to take our loneliness away." After years of longing, it was suddenly happening to him, but his priestly formation and living meant that he didn't have the emotional maturity to realize it was not, in fact, mutual in the way he hoped it might be or an understanding of how all relationships are built on compromise not dominance.

While this friendship had its own private dynamics, it is not uncommon to have a powerful falling-in-love experience while moving from one way of life to another. Neither is it unusual for someone during a time of readjustment to project the complicated needs and desires of their own vulnerability onto the object of their attraction, especially if the other person, perhaps inexperienced in relationships, suddenly feels more confident, even elevated, in the company of an impressive, older friend. However, this can deceive the needier person into believing the attraction is mutual because everything he ever longed for is in his orbit every day—and he wants more and more to satiate a demand the other cannot possibly live up to because of inexperience, confusion, and, ultimately, fear.

Of course, this may not have been the psychological scenario for Henri and Nathan, and it would not be anybody else's business except for the fact that one of the world's most renowned spiritual authors decided to write about it. Henri's journal entries about his rapport with Nathan are astonishingly revealing in their emotional intensity—almost like a teenager sharing with everyone the joys of first love—but apparently Henri wore even more of his heart on his sleeve in the first draft. This does raise a question concerning the extent to which Henri considered Nathan's feelings when preparing his diary for publication. With advice from others in the community, Nathan needed to withdraw slowly and firmly. Henri, noted for his sensitivity over the slightest rejection, was bound to take this distancing as badly as possible. He felt abandoned and worthless, unable to function and therefore at a loss to integrate all that was happening to him.

We can trace the changes in Henri's emotional and psychological responses around this time by studying more unpublished correspondence from him to Michael Harank. Here, on blank paper, writing nine months after his previous letter, the tone has changed notably as he laments the disintegration of his friendship with Nathan:

May '87

Dear Michael,

Just another note to stay in touch. I think of you and wished [*sic*] we could be together. I feel very needy, lonely, depressed and grieving for the loss of my friendship with Nathan. I understand in my mind the need for distance, but my heart cannot accept it easily. In fact I keep waking up at night agonizing about unanswerable questions such as "Why did this happen?" "What did I do wrong?" etc.

But I find much support from Jean Vanier with whom I have been completely open. He gives me some safe space to express my anguish. So don't worry about me. Just know that I miss you and wished [*sic*] I could cry a little with you and feel your presence—

I pray for you and hope your exams went well.

Love Henri

Michael Harank noted how the letter disclosed that the intensity of Henri's emotional landscape had radically altered since the last time he wrote. It had seemed much like he was climbing a mountain, with the vigorous energy he felt from living at L'Arche and the unmistakable passion that comes with "falling in love." But Henri's heart had been broken, and the friendship now required a physical separation and distance. He had reached a vital and visionary pinnacle of a possible loving friendship or relationship, said Michael, and then was abruptly plunged into a freefall of desperation and abandonment evoking powerful feelings of being "needy, lonely, depressed and grieving." It was apparent to Michael, at the time, that Henri felt humanly helpless and terribly wounded. True friendship at such a desperate, lonely moment required a comforting presence. This is what he gained from the support of Jean Vanier and from friends who could receive his deepest desire to "cry with you and feel your presence." Michael, too, had always offered Henri his support.

Later that month, Michael received a card from Italy:

Thursday May '87

Dear Michael, Many greetings from Rome. I think of you and pray for you especially during this time of separation from Benedict. I admire your inner strength and freedom. I am still experiencing much darkness and anguish. Sometimes it seems that there is no way out of the inner sense of rejection, self-doubt and being abandoned. I hope and pray that this crisis will lead me to a deeper faith and stronger faith in Jesus. Pray for me. Love Henri.

"Here is the lingering, weary, dark night of the broken heart and soul wound that continued to burden Henri," said Michael Harank. "His prayer to receive a 'deeper' and 'stronger' faith in Jesus would now be inseparable from his existential experience of utter brokenness. Now he could celebrate Mass among members of L'Arche community, knowing and feeling more deeply than ever the eucharistic words 'broken for you.' The nourishment of the Eucharist was now intimately connected to the brokenness he felt so deeply."

Living in a community of broken people who understood the meaning of fragmentation and woundedness in different incarnational ways, Henri had been forced to confront the contradictions and paradoxes of his life. He had been trying to hold together the different strands, but they were being stretched to breaking point and beyond. Henri suffered a total collapse of strength and energy, retaining, however, the salvific gift of writing. Close friends who cared for Henri during his long, dark night remembered that he turned up one day in Surrey, Britain, with an icon of St. George and the Dragon, telling them, "I am coming here to do battle." The brown-bordered holy image with a red background showed the saint on a white horse spearing the enemy through its mouth. It became a daily focus of what this tormented mystic felt he was up against. At the time, he probably saw his sexuality as a dark, menacing force. The friends came to recognize that Henri was a man torn between two powerful realities in his life, a combat between *being* and *need*. The question that constantly preoccupied him was whether he should abandon what he thought was his calling because of his need. On the one hand, he believed he had a vocation to the priesthood; on the other, he was a person with strong human needs. He knew that, as a priest who loved to celebrate the Eucharist every day, he was obliged to be celibate, but at the same time, at the point of his need, he was a very human person strongly drawn and attracted to others in terms of his brokenness, yearnings, and sexuality. So, the dilemma was stark: should he remain in the priesthood or leave, so that the ache inside him could be healed and the need fulfilled? He was getting to know gay people whose worldview contrasted strikingly from his more reserved, traditional stance. Yet the friendships made a huge impression on him because he could see how happy and contented his gay pals had become. While he was unquestionably attracted to the choices they had made, he nevertheless felt disturbed and unsettled at the thought of following suit. So, when discussing the prospects before him with his friends and guides, he could only express his frustration in confessional language, using such words as *anguish* or *guilt*. Beneath the wounded child and the sexual longings was a sense of calling that undergirded his entire life. "You could always call Henri to faithfulness, a term he used again and again," the guides said. The wound of being, the wound of love, and the wound of needing to know he was loved, which could be traced back to the playpen, remained center stage in the drama of his life. The wounds were both the incredible strength and glory of his life, but also the agony. They had become so entrenched that they could take obsessive forms. At one level, they were a huge creative force, but at another, they betrayed the character of weakness and brokenness.

Although Henri did not undergo psychotherapy as systematically as many North Americans did during the last decades of the twentieth century, he saw psychiatrists or psychologists occasionally but apparently never stayed with a therapist for long-term treatment. However, nothing could have prepared him for the gradual deterioration in his mental health at Daybreak, which reached crisis point in December 1987, only sixteen months after he joined the community. He was not the first Christian mystic to suffer catastrophic mental health issues. A breakdown can occur when a major decision has been made but when it is not in alignment with every facet of the personality. Leaving the more comfortable world of academia and going to L'Arche triggered a massive crisis. Community living required accountability, stability, commitment, self-revelation, and loving others daily in a practical rather than theoretical way.

After Henri agreed to go to L'Arche and, at the same time, met Nathan who stimulated his own need to love and be loved, he was confronted with the need for huge internal changes within himself, which eventually led to a total breakdown. The darkest period of Henri's life, then, was this period before he went into therapy at Manitoba. For Henri, this was not just a dark night of the soul but a dark night of everything—of the spirit, at the point of his own being, desires, longings, and sexuality, his own calling, and his work. But he did not lose his faith because he remained faithful to the Word, saying the office, celebrating the Eucharist— and writing. Even though he hardly had the energy to drag himself out of bed some mornings, he still had the energy to write, and it was a salvation to him to keep on doing that. In the maelstrom of despair and agony, he was open and was given to being called to faithfulness. He wanted to live what he wrote about, knowing all the while he was wounded and that what he was enduring was the most terrifying nightmare for him. He longed to find God in it but had no clue where God could be located. God was absent from him in it. "St. Paul spoke of sacrificing oneself on the altar of your brother and sister's faith," the friends said. "That's right where he was. He was being held by other people and it was a bleak time." Always impassioned, Henri naturally experienced the darkness enveloping him as intense. Furthermore, his spiritual awareness and articulation of the issues meant the darkness was darker for him because he knew exactly what was at stake. His brokenness was not unusual, but the fruit or expression of it was magnified because of who he was, and he had very little space to work it out.

The L'Arche community was open and supportive, but this was far beyond anything they or he had ever experienced. Henri visited a friend who was a psychiatrist and talked through his issues. He also consulted two psychiatrists at a nearby therapy center, but Henri soon realized that, if he were treated only as a psychological person, he would not get through what was happening to him. He needed both emotional and spiritual support. The questions in his mind revolved around where he could receive that support, who could interpret what was happening, who could name what needed to be named, and what therapist or spiritual disciplines would be most effective in healing. Eventually, he was recommended Homes for Growth in Winnipeg, Manitoba. This was a community living in several houses that welcomed people who were fragile or who needed to grow through a pain or specific problem. Some of the staff had specific training, others did not, but they were always available to people staying there.

Henri lived in a house with four or five others. Some joined in community events, but he decided not to. However, he did various exercises and had the Blessed Sacrament in his room in front of which he would pray every day. During the first months, this meant lying on the floor in front of it crying out in anguish. He saw his guides every day—a man and a woman—and underwent treatment that combined spiritual direction with psychotherapy. A friend who learned about those six months directly from Henri shared what he remembered of the conversation:

> One of his therapists offered him a body-centered therapy that he found extraordinarily helpful, affirming, and, on some level, therapeutic. Being able to be held physically in a nonsexual way was something that worked for him and responded to a craving within him. It would take place, for comfort's sake, on a bed in an office. Henri would be held by a therapist who was a man. Both were fully clothed. In the arms of his therapist, there was a primal state. He would be held very tightly and, in that context, weep, scream, writhe, and be caressed. It sounded as though he could do all the things that a small child might do. To be held in that way, unconditionally, with immense nurture and tenderness, was for him very healing.
>
> I would conjecture that he began to understand better what had brought him to this crash period in his life, and he could now more hopefully try to heal the relationship that had troubled him. I would not say that he had it all figured out, and he didn't see that as a failure. There was an openness to continuing to go forward. Some elements of life were still very much a mystery. There was still a vulnerability there with the part of him that had collapsed, and after returning to Daybreak, he still went back to Winnipeg for follow-up visits. This got him through what was probably the most significant emotional crisis of his life. But it did not bring him to a state of enlightenment.

As Henri showed signs of improvement, writing became a salvation for him. The truth was that he couldn't do anything else, was unable to see people, and did not want to talk to others about what was happening to him, so he felt closeted. Remarkably, during these unthinkably forlorn months, Henri managed to keep his head above water by working on *The Return of the Prodigal Son*. Like the medieval mystics whose physical ailments did not debilitate but drew them into new heights of awareness of God, Henri's spiritual writing is arguably at its most perceptive during this period. (A comparison might also be made with Vincent van Gogh, who believed the act of painting would help him recover his mental equilibrium after mutilating his ear following a vicious argument with Paul Gauguin in Arles). Henri also kept a journal of spiritual imperatives that eventually became *The Inner Voice of Love*. Here, Henri writes about the need to find the origins of his loneliness, recognizing that its pain might be rooted in his deepest vocation and even lead him to a knowledge of God's love:

> When you run away from it, your loneliness does not really diminish; you simply force it out of your mind temporarily. When you start dwelling in it, your feelings only become stronger, and you slip into depression.
>
> The spiritual task is not to escape your loneliness, not to let yourself drown in it, but to find its source. This is not so easy to do, but when you can somehow identify the place from which these feelings emerge, they will lose some of their power over you.[1]

Henri was able to return to Daybreak as pastor, but the restoration of the friendship with Nathan had to proceed slowly as both men initially kept their distance and knew that inner healing would take a long time. It led to the embracing of what Henri had already termed "the second loneliness" with Jesus in community, which he found "much, much harder" to live than the loneliness that resulted from physical or emotional isolation. "There is nothing charming or romantic about it," he writes. "It is dark agony. It is following

Jesus to a completely unknown place. It is being emptied out on the cross and having to wait for new life in naked faith."[2]

Michael Harank felt that, because of the "refining furnace" of a total breakdown, Henri was able to emerge "with a little more humility about who he was in the world" as he began to become more aware of the contradictions of his life, especially in the area of sexuality. "He was not a peaceful person, but when his friends offered him a little wine and a lot of love, he would take off his medieval church armor, let down his defenses, which were enormous, and relax a little; then he would embody a quality of presence that was always a delight to be in the presence of." Michael told me that he believed his friend had felt "very deeply" the absence of God's unconditional love for him at different times in his life, a void not unknown to the great mystics of history. Nonetheless, Michael Harank also made the point that, after an illuminating experience, such people tended to live with a lighter, relaxed response to the world, no longer burdened by the weight of the world's suffering because their encounter had also been an insight into the truth that God carried it all. The genuine mystics, then, exhibited a certain quality of life and a distinct quality of attention that sustained their subsequent religious practices. Henri, however, was "the apostle of anxiety and alienation," knowing well the landscape and theology of those human emotions. "I don't think he was really able to accept the unconditional love of God because he could not accept the unconditional human quality of who he was until the last three or four years of his life."

7

UNITY OF SOULS

The reward of friendship is itself.

—Aelred of Rievaulx

Henri Nouwen believed friendship was one of the greatest gifts a human being could receive, a bond stronger than sexual union could create and deeper than a shared fate could solidify. It could even be more intimate than marriage or community. "Friendship is being with the other in joy and sorrow, even when we cannot increase the joy or decrease the sorrow," he writes. "It is a unity of souls that gives nobility and sincerity to love. Friendship makes all of life shine brightly. Blessed are those who lay down their lives for their friends."[1] These carefully chosen words could perhaps only have been written by someone who had experienced the absence of friendship. It is possible that he discovered that the precious nature of friendship could only be defined and valued during times of aloneness or hurt. Henri had more friends than many people, yet at the same time could feel loneliness and rejection more acutely than most.

Many readers of Henri's books believed he understood their

issues so remarkably in print that he was already a friend of theirs. Such was the power of his writing that some wrote him long letters, perhaps secretly hoping that somehow a friendship would flow from their correspondence. The truth is that it *was* possible to be a fan of Henri Nouwen and then to become a close friend of his. One young man was so influenced by Henri's books and articles on pastoral care that his one desire in life was not just to meet his spiritual hero but to spend a week with him. At the time, Frank Hamilton was a Presbyterian minister barely thirty years old, twenty years younger than Henri. But investing in the motto "Nothing ventured, nothing gained," he began to write letters and followed them up with a call to Henri's secretary who, while friendly, did not hold out much hope that Frank would be able to realize his dream. "I settled for crumbs from his table," said Frank, "knowing that, if Henri Nouwen was all he appeared to be from his books, he wouldn't reject me. When eventually I got to speak to him, he tried to put me off, but after two further calls, I bought an airline ticket to Boston and spent a few days in his home. We prayed and reflected on the scriptures together three hours a day. He came away three days later educationally and spiritually fulfilled." One evening, Henri said to him, "Frank, every week I receive at least fifty letters, like the ones you sent me, every week, but I'm too busy to see the people who write them." Frank wondered why he had been successful and learned it was because of his persistence. "You taught me the true meaning of the word *importunity*," Henri told him. It was an allusion to the persistent widow in the parable of the unjust judge (Luke 18:1–8). "You would not be put off. You kept coming back, even offering to meet me in Peru. You went for it and got it."

Throughout the 1980s, Henri was Frank's spiritual director. They tried to meet at least five times a year. One day, out of the blue, Henri told Frank that he didn't need him as his spiritual directee any longer. Frank's heart sank and found himself at a total loss for words. Then, in a more intimate tone, Henri went on,

"Frank, I need a friend and spiritual confidant. I have observed you for the past nine years and feel I can trust you. I could get a thousand spiritual directees. But I need a friend and I am inviting you to friendship with me." But Frank didn't give Henri the instant response he was probably hoping for. He could only let him know in time because he needed to pray about it. "I knew Henri well enough to understand the demands of being his friend," Frank said. "I would need to be available 24/7 to discuss whatever Henri needed to discuss, travel with him to events, proofread each book prior to publication, and chauffeur him. Henri was not proficient at driving, and I probably extended his life by fulfilling that role. In short, I knew he was asking for a friend and occasional secretary. As well as around-the-clock availability, being Henri's friend would require absolute honesty and a willingness to challenge him." That day, though, Henri's impatience (and fear of rejection) got the better of him. "When will you let me know?" he demanded. Coolly, Frank replied, "One year from today. I really need a year to pray about this." Dumbfounded and clearly downhearted, Henri asked why such a long period of discernment was necessary. It was simple: Frank needed to seek God's will. Believe it or not, a year to the day, Frank returned to Daybreak, as promised, and was met by an anxious Henri at the door. Greeting Frank with a hug, he asked immediately, "Well?" Frank told him he was humbled by the request and would gladly accept the invitation.

As close friend and spiritual confidant, Frank Hamilton was in a privileged position to witness the human side of his spiritual director, experiencing him as a humble companion if at times splenetic. Frank remembered Henri being an early riser, bounding out of bed at six to shower, dress, and pray in the chapel at Daybreak. Breakfast consisted of toasted breads, butter, jelly, yogurt, and coffee. Sometimes there would be bacon and eggs. Over the meal, Henri would usually discuss the Scripture readings for the day with those joining him around the table. Frank was initially taken aback by the personal wardrobe of the international author who might be mixing with White House senators one day and the likes of Mother Teresa the next. "I was impressed that a man of Henri's stature with his extensive travel schedule would have such a limited wardrobe, but clothes were not important to him," he said. "Henri owned twelve white Oxford shirts, twelve blue Oxford shirts, three pairs of navy blue pants, one pair of black pants, one cashmere sweater, and one suit."

One of Frank's responsibilities was to discuss with Henri his upcoming books. Henri's publisher in San Francisco was Harper Collins, so when Frank (who became a U.S. Air Force chaplain) was assigned to Beale Air Force Base, some ninety miles from San Francisco, he would meet Henri at Holy Redeemer Retreat Center in Oakland. The following day, they would have lunch with a publishing representative. "The first time this happened, Henri and the HarperCollins representative gave me full authority to read and edit all of his writings," Frank told me. "In fifteen years, I only made three corrections to Henri's grammar or spelling. Henri was insistent on using American grammar and spelling, not European.

"When Henri visited me at the Air Force base, he and the phone were inseparable. I could expect $900 phone bills with the calls he made to Russia, the Ukraine, South America, the Vatican, India, and other far-flung places. Henri always reimbursed me for the calls, but I was always amazed at the scope of his friends and influence. Henri had his own travel agent and changed his schedule often. Many a time, oblivious of time zones, Henri would call me in the middle of the night and express his loneliness. I remember when Henri received an award in Detroit. He phoned me at three in the morning and told me he was lonely. I remember him saying, 'Here I am in a suite, in one of the finest hotels in Detroit, and I have no one to share this experience with.'"

"Whenever Henri received an international guest and I was present, he would insist that English be spoken so that I could participate in the conversation. Only on a very few occasions would Henri say, 'Frank, please excuse us, but we must speak

Dutch, German, or whatever because of the technicalities we are discussing.' I was always amazed how much I could understand when they switched languages because so many of our theological words originated in Latin. Henri was always receiving unexpected guests. One day, two Dutch men unexpectedly knocked on his door for a spiritual conversation. Henri graciously received them and offered them refreshments along with lively conversation. When the visit was over, the guests insisted on helping me wash the dishes. When Henri joined in, one of them said, 'Henri will never wash my dirty dish.' I advised the guests that Henri would be hurt if he were to be excluded from this task."

Although Henri might absentmindedly interrupt other people's private meetings at whim, he himself did not like to be disturbed while working—yet another paradox of his life and times. One day, he and Frank were concentrating hard on a project in the office when his secretary knocked on his door and excitedly announced, "Henri, the First Lady is on the telephone from the White House." There was no response, so she tried again—and again. Hillary Clinton was keen to speak to the author because *The Return of the Prodigal Son* had helped her through some difficult times. She wanted to tell him so, perhaps even hoping to meet him. In desperation, the secretary knocked a fourth time, then opened the door and urged Henri to take the call from the wife of the president of the United States. Henri looked up and replied phlegmatically, "Tell Mrs. Clinton that I am with Frank right now and I will call her back in ten minutes." That is how the famous spiritual author kept the First Lady waiting. Henri was a firm believer that everyone was created equally, and everyone was equally important. It made Frank realize how Henri really cared for him and others. If he was giving attention to somebody, that person was more important than anyone else—even the wife of the president of the United States.

Frank would listen intently as Henri shared aspects of his life, like how he felt alienated and clumsy on the sports field.

He once said during a baseball game at Daybreak, "My body is not my friend in sports." Frank remembered him speaking of the Nazi occupation of Holland during his childhood, and Frank concluded that this might also have been a factor in Henri's needing to feel protected and safe as a young boy. He remembered Henri telling him that, when he was about ten, his mother was always going out of her way to be kind to the Nazis who would turn up at Dutch homes at dinner time to take away from the family the food they had prepared to eat. "This didn't occur at the Nouwen household," Frank said. "Henri attributed this to his mother's kindness to these people, which stood out from the contempt they received at other Dutch homes." Henri's father had been a forward planner. In the event of the Nazis becoming more aggressive, taking people off to concentration camps, he had built several trunks with fake bottoms so that the family could hide inside should the house be searched. Frank also remembered Henri speaking about how his parents would take their bicycles (without any rubber tires) and ride as far as ten miles to find food for the family.

During the time they spent together over the years, the two friends shared stories of their upbringings and the way their vocations to minister had evolved. Frank recollected, in particular, the "great respect and compassion" that Henri had shown to people living with HIV and AIDS. "Henri had promised the Lucey family in California that he would be present when Rose's son, John, passed away. He was notified at 3:00 a.m. that he should depart Harvard and fly to San Francisco to be alongside the family. Although Henri had scheduled classes to teach at Harvard, he put friendship first and left immediately to support the family and conduct the funeral service."

TRAVELING WITH HENRI

Naturally, people were curious to know what it was like being so close to such a spiritual and famous individual. One of the ways

Frank processed their questions was to look at what grounded his friend. "Henri was first and foremost a man of prayer who relied on the Eucharist and the Holy Scriptures to nourish his soul," he said. "Henri saw prayer as being with God. For him, theology was always talking with God. Henri faithfully prayed the Liturgy of the Hours. We prayed it together ourselves, and had discursive prayer. Henri also spent many hours in adoration of the Blessed Sacrament and praying the Rosary. When Henri was praying in silence, I could see that he was in ecstasy. There is no other word to describe it." Frank's recollection is redolent of St. Isaac of Nineveh, who said, "The love of God is fiery by nature, and when it descends in an extraordinary degree onto a person, it throws that soul into ecstasy."[2]

Frank pointed out that all religions had mystics who attempted and longed to give meaning to the mystery of God. "Henri was there seeing the mystery of God, then interpreting it for those who could not understand it," he explained. "The mystic in Henri took him from the childhood chapel in the attic of his house in Holland, to places all over the world of both grandeur and poverty, and finally to the grave. These places Henri went to were the mystic's search for God, not as ends in themselves, but at the same time also helping others in their search for God. Henri the mystic was a channel for God's truth to speak to our hearts.

"In view of Henri's challenges with his father, over the course of two years he prayed the five decades of the Rosary using the words 'You are my Son, the Beloved, in whom I am well pleased' instead of saying 'Hail Mary, full of grace….' That was 'coming home' to Henri, and not long afterwards his father presented him with an icon which to Henri symbolized a long-awaited affirmation which Henri understood not only as the Father's love but also his own father's love."

According to Frank Hamilton, "Talking with Henri was filled with new ideas about the Church, the pope, social justice, and how the U.S. Senate's actions affect the world. People sent him books to review and he would tell me what the books were about and how he would critique them. He shared his opinion and asked me for mine. Often, I would sit with Henri and a little voice would go off inside of me which would say, 'Why are you here? How did you get into the heart of this prominent theologian and sit here listening to his great words and thoughts? What have you to offer this man Henri? Will Henri discover that you have a simple mind and tire of you?' But with these self-doubts came the realization that Henri loved me—and loved me unconditionally. He loved and valued me deeply, and could see beyond barriers."

The world-renowned author was highly educated and loved learning and sharing his knowledge. A fluency in several languages, including Latin, provided an entrée into diverse cultures of the world. When writing a book, he utilized all these resources. Frank remembered how, over the course of two years, Henri formulated his views on the Eucharist. "He wanted to look at the host being taken, blessed, broken, and distributed at the Mass. I listened to Henri as he discussed and produced the book *Can You Drink the Cup?* When it was published, it became my favorite book, although at the time Henri was writing it, I could not conceptualize what he was trying to convey."

During my conversations with Frank, the minor details also sprang to mind—how, before supper, Henri had liked a glass of red wine, accompanied by some crackers and cheeses, and how, at other times, he would snack on large chocolate chip cookies. Henri's "European" love of flowers was also a talking point. "He loved to receive flowers and would often gaze at them for long periods of time," said Frank. "When he himself sent them, he would often go into great detail with the florist as to how the flowers should look and be arranged in the vase. One morning, Henri was on the telephone, ordering flowers and dictating the words for the card. They were a gift for a gay author who lived in California. After the call ended, Henri said, 'I just cannot believe it—I heard on the news that he was hospitalized in Los Angeles, and I wanted to give him flowers to cheer his day.' Flowers and people cheered Henri's day."

Henri and Frank liked to relax on their holidays, which were not without incident. Once, while traveling to a Camaldolese monastery in Big Sur, California, they stopped off at a Carmelite monastery in Carmel to leave a gift for one of the nuns. "When we arrived at the monastery, we rang the bell and waited for one of the sisters to answer the door," Frank recalled. "As we waited, we could hear water gushing inside. We rang the bell a couple more times and finally an out-of-breath sister arrived at the door. Henri introduced himself by saying, 'Hello, I am Henri Nouwen of the Daybreak community and I am…' Abruptly interrupting him, the sister retorted, 'I know of Henri Nouwen, but this is no time to talk about him. We are having a flood and I thought you were someone important like the plumber.' With that, she slammed the door. I doubled over with laughter as Henri's whole body reaction was one of: 'Don't you know who I am? I am Henri Nouwen and I have been asked to bring a gift to one of the sisters.' Henri and I waited a few more minutes. Then the plumber arrived and rang the bell. He was warmly received. With that, the door was slammed shut again in our faces. Henri felt it was probably not a good day to call. As we were leaving, one of the sisters came to the door and said they were having plumbing problems but if we could wait… Henri decided we should return another day, so we told her we were continuing to Big Sur. The next day, he received a handwritten letter from Mother Superior profusely apologizing for the incident and inviting him to call in on his return journey. Henri accepted her apology and invitation. He even offered to give a spiritual meditation to the sisters."

Frank joined Henri on a visit to Germany where they traveled with a flying trapeze troupe about which Henri planned to write a book, as I will explain in chapter 9. One of Frank's jobs was to photograph the daring acts for the project. It involved climbing fifty feet up a twelve-inch-wide ladder to the top of the king pole where, from a small platform, he captured the action. On one of their days off, they were invited by a local priest to take part in a service and religious procession around a heavily wooded park in Dortmund. Not quite sure of what to expect, they decided to carry with them two plastic sacks of dirty laundry, which a circus friend had offered to wash for them afterward. But they couldn't find the event through all the trees and began to search desperately. In their haste, Frank tripped on a bridge, ripped his trousers, and badly hurt his knee. Blood began to seep through the material, then one of the bags ripped open, exposing the soiled apparel. By the time they eventually located the service and were ushered unceremoniously onto a bench, the third reading was well underway. After receiving holy communion, the priest invited them, as clergy, to walk near the front of the procession, behind the blessed relics, which were under a canopy, and ahead of the city's Lord Mayor. The hapless pair commenced the forty-five-minute parade, one bloodied hand holding the torn bag of washing as best it could with an embarrassed Frank all the while fearing that news cameras might well capture the unholy sight or that the mayor might be forced to pick up anything that fell out. It was at that point that Frank turned to Henri and whispered, "I guess we are invited to march in God's Parade, even with our dirty laundry," to which Henri retorted, "That's the point."

In March 1996, Henri and Frank met in New Mexico, having not seen each other for seven months. They stayed a week in Santa Fe at the house of friends who had gone away. Their aim was to read, write, talk, and pray, as well as explore one of the most historic corners of the United States. They were immediately impressed by the cultural intermingling of the Pueblo Indians, the Hispanics, and the Anglos. Henri was overwhelmed by the beauty of the Indian jewelry and the black-on-black pottery, though was less responsive to the modern art inspired by the state's turbulent past, clear sunlight, rich flora, desertscapes, and adobe houses. A few days later, they drove through the desert to the Church of Chimayó. The small adobe building with two towers and a walled-in courtyard was known as the Lourdes of America. Every year, nearly three hundred thousand pilgrims pray for peace or seek healing there. A "miraculous crucifix," discovered in 1810, forms the center of the shrine. An adjacent room contains a small well where people can cross themselves with "holy dirt." Writing of the experience, Henri the mystic says they were engulfed by an atmosphere of prayer. "You could feel that for more than a century and a half people had filled this intimate space with their cries, tears, and words of thanks and praise. The crucifix on the main altar surrounded by a reredos of painted symbols is deeply moving. The face of Christ is gentle and loving even in his agony. We prayed for a while and went to the El Pozito, where people were kneeling and crossing themselves with the dry sand."[3]

Several days later, it was still dark when Henri and Frank left for the airport. They prayed together en route. Although Henri always wanted farewells to be special, he did not find them painless. On the way to the gate, he started to complain. It was as though a demon was invading him and trying to destroy their good week together. According to Henri's account in *Sabbatical Journey* (being a friend of Henri inevitably meant that, sooner or later, you would end up in print), Frank didn't want coffee or food and seemed rather flat, overly concerned with getting his boarding pass and calling friends. "Suddenly, I had the experience of being left alone. I felt as though we were just going through the motions, and that, in reality, Frank wanted to be by himself."[4] Aware that this was mostly projection on his part, Henri was nonetheless unable to contain himself. "Where are you?" he asked Frank. "You are no longer here. I had hoped we could have a good chat and a warm farewell. I feel as if you are happy that the vacation is over." Reacting strongly, Frank told Henri not to deny the good week they had lived together: "Don't ruin it all. Yes, I did have to make a phone call, and I didn't want to drink coffee, but you make a lot out of nothing. I just find it hard to talk in airports."[5]

Frank's reaction both embarrassed and saddened Henri. Before his plane left, he was able to thank Frank for his friendship, but still felt disappointed and all the way back to Toronto "kept thinking about my inability to step through my feelings."[6] When Frank called him later, Henri asked for forgiveness. The conversation helped him reclaim the good week they had shared. The following day—six months before his death—Henri wrote in his journal that his short stay in New Mexico had given him a glimpse of the permanent reality shining through the impermanence of all created things:

> The days in Santa Fe, simple and unpretentious as they were, revealed to me in a new way the beauty of life. Friendship, art, nature, history, and the tangible presence of the immanent as well as transcendent love of God filled me with gratitude for being alive and being alive with others.[7]

When Henri died a few months later, Frank was on a military deployment in Haiti and did not have any civilian clothes with him. "I had my office send my suit to Canada, but it did not arrive in time, so I was privileged to wear Henri's only suit to his funeral. I was also a pallbearer. The family asked me to sit with them and I did. Michael Harank and I provided around twenty-two prayers for the funeral mass intercessions."

Speaking to me the day before he left for Russia to see for the first time Rembrandt's painting "The Return of the Prodigal Son," about which his friend had written so perceptively, Frank Hamilton talked about the impact Henri's death had made on him. "It was the most significant loss I have ever had," he said. "I knew that, in order to be faithful to Henri and my own theology, my reaction could not mock all that Henri had stood for. Henri had set a standard of prayer and trust I knew I had to be faithful to and honor all that Henri had given me for the rest of my life.

Henri's death was a spiritual experience for me. It was more than losing a friend and spiritual confidant. It was losing the man who had interpreted the difficulties of my life and helped me resolve them. I was twenty years younger. I am now a year older than the age Henri was when he died. I am a very private man and I am speaking now because I want Henri's memory, as well as his work and spirituality, to be passed on to another generation. Those of us who knew him are getting fewer every day. Perhaps I can be a fresh voice and one that speaks to that younger generation who need to discover him.

"I knew I was going around with a holy man, and an important man, but I would be careful how I interacted with him because of his fragility. He was a spiritual leader and God talked to him. He opened new possibilities for me but also for his reading public. I feel privileged that Henri chose to include me and share the very deep parts of his life. He taught me how to pray, to think, to relate to people, and to listen.

"Henri displayed the characteristics of a mystic in being a mediator between God and a thirsting people."

8

PUBLIC AND PRIVATE

Worldly honors are acceptable to him who receives them indifferently.

—Francis de Sales

When a diocesan bishop invited Henri Nouwen to lead a retreat, the world-famous guide of souls checked his diary and didn't hesitate to agree. Many who turned up were awestruck by how he brought God alive for them. Before people returned home, the bishop presented their illustrious host with a silver medallion that had the writer's own image imprinted on it and an inscription that read, "Henri Nouwen—Master of the Spiritual Life." Never one to be lured into romanticism or the trappings of fame, Henri paused, peered at the gift and, with the timing of a true professional, looked up and asked, "Didn't you know I was going for the gold?" The retreatants tittered out of embarrassment, not knowing how to react, but it was a gesture of genuine modesty from a man who neither desired to be stalked as a personality, nor wished to be reverenced as a guru. He discouraged adoring responses wherever he went, although not always successfully. As he tried to make clear, time and again, he had a calling to share his life with others, not laud it over them. He tried to dodge those devotees queuing solely to pay homage, but they were not easy to avoid.

Many of the great Christian mystics, about whom stories and myths swiftly accumulated, achieved popularity only after their deaths and, in some cases, a long time afterward. It was different for Henri. People who met him during his lifetime often remarked that they were in the presence of a man who seemed close to God. Was this a form of spiritual hero worship or a legitimate divine encounter? With Henri, there was none of the celebrity self-importance or aloofness usually associated with men and women driven by their own fame. While Henri liked to be genuinely appreciated in religious circles and enjoyed the recognition when he was noticed in a new milieu, he was more interested in the life of the person approaching him than he was listening to a litany of platitudes about his books. *American Idol* was not his style.

Nevertheless, it needs to be said that, because there had never really been a spiritual writer like Henri—roaming the planet and touching people's hearts—he was inundated with fan mail, and it was not uncommon for hitchhikers to turn up at Daybreak because of him. Here was an author who used memorable images drawn from life rather than religion, and readers were not slow in identifying themselves in the stories he told about himself. He possessed the uncanny skill of making his audience feel that he was speaking directly to their hearts and comprehending their needs as no one had understood them before. While this was never a psychological trick, it was something of an illusion, of course, because he was really responding to the common human search for love and belonging: "What is most personal is most universal," as the American psychologist Carl Rogers put it. In much the same way, when people who met him in person opened up to him, he listened with such penetrating intensity that they felt they were the only ones who mattered. This pastoral gift, while, again, utterly authentic, could create problems if the person he were counseling interpreted the spiritual guidance as something more emotionally intimate than he had intended. One tearful woman told me how she and Henri had grown so close that he was on the point of leaving the Roman Catholic priesthood to marry her. This was not the only delusion I encountered on my journey to discover the real Henri whose magnetic charm and soul-reading had the charismatic power to infatuate people of more mature years— and sometimes people of less. Everyone seemed to love him at some level, perhaps quietly hoping they were the only ones.

The Quaker author Parker Palmer pointed out that readers made "terrific projections" upon writers. "They read in our books some kind of mastery over subjects that is about the opposite of what is true," he told me. "I think the reason one writes about something is because one is still wrestling with it. In that sense, Henri was writing to himself. I think if you write about something that you have totally mastered you get bored with it and it is probably going to be a boring book. Henri's books were deeply engrossing and engaging precisely because they came out of the ongoing wrestling match with his own life. In that sense, he practiced what he preached, and what he preached was the struggle, sometimes the anguish, sometimes the joy, but always a very energetic set of ideas that he was clearly living and writing."

When Henri was taking part in a national tour, speaking about Central America and specifically Nicaragua, Chris Glaser went to hear him at a huge church, filled to capacity, in Pasadena, California. "It was on this occasion that I realized Henri had become a celebrity," he said. "The sanctuary was electric with anticipation and, when he appeared, I heard the nearest thing to a collective gasp of excitement I have ever heard. Whispers of 'there he is!' and 'that's him!' passed through the crowd as if he were a rock star ascending the stage. And boy, did he deliver! Without notes, he kept us spellbound for an hour. Afterward, when he saw me over the heads of the many clamoring to shake his hand or have him sign books, he waved to me and shouted for me not to leave until everything was over. Henri satisfied the last autograph seeker, who apologized but nonetheless handed him fifteen books to sign. Later, out of earshot, he said to me, 'I tell them not to have my books at events because I spend all my time signing and I don't really get to meet people.'"

Kevin Dwyer told me that he called him in California from the east coast, saying, "I just got through signing a zillion books. I'm very lonely right now. I'm in my hotel room and I don't know anybody. I'm very sad." He was about to cry, said Kevin. "To me, that shed light on the fact that his writings were a curse as well as a blessing. He didn't say that personally but there was this constant asking to be with friends who accepted him as Henri. I remember once, when he had celebrated Mass with us, he put his arm around me and said, 'It's so good to have people in my life who don't see me as a famous writer, who see me as I am.' This is what he was hungry for. My memories of him are ones of touch when he would put his strong hands on the back of your neck or your shoulder. He was a powerful person. When he hugged you, you knew you were being hugged by somebody who really wanted communion with another human being."

There was always a brittle tension between privacy and public connection in Henri's life. He fell in love with the serenity of the old Spanish-style retreat center that Kevin ran and asked that no one be told he was there, but then he would walk around the complex saying, "Hi, I'm Henri Nouwen." By all accounts, he could not protect himself from meeting people, sharing who he was, and getting to know them. It was usually a two-way process. So, Henri seems to have had an ambiguous attitude toward his own fame. Part of him yearned for quiet places where he could discard the mantle of being a popular writer; yet he might also attend Mass at a nearby church where he was guaranteed anonymity, only to approach the parish priest at the end of the service and introduce himself. He could, however, appear slightly surprised and disappointed if the priest responded by providing his own name without any evident indication of recognizing the magic words "Henri Nouwen." At the height of his fame, Henri would receive invitations to speak to religious communities throughout the United States. He could have expected at least 150 dollars as a stipend for the talk and 500 dollars would not have been excessive in view of his spiritual stature. Yet sometimes he would receive only the cost of his flight, but naturally he wasn't a person to insist on payment.

As someone who valued privacy to regenerate, as he had so little of it, Henri was his own worst enemy at times. After a visit to Texas, where he had led a church workshop and given a public talk, he drove with friends to a secluded house for a weekend of quiet reading, writing, walking, and eating together. In Henri's frenzied world, this was a rare oasis of peace and relaxation, but much to the chagrin of the host, Henri had already given out the telephone number to a bevy of people. He insisted on sleeping in the room by the telephone, which rang the entire time, and when it wasn't ringing, Henri was dialing out. It was a compulsion he failed to conquer and clearly symptomatic of his persistent need to make contact.

Henri Nouwen's attitude to fame was often ambiguous. In *A Cry for Mercy*, he pleads, "O Lord, I am self-centered, concerned about myself, my career, my future, my name and fame. Often I even feel that I use you for my own advantage." This is not a prayer to pass over in haste, for Henri is confessing here that his life as a popular writer about God may actually be a means of enhancing his own reputation in the eyes of the world. He thinks he is doing it for himself and not God. This must surely relate to his primal wound of needing admiration, and it also raises the question of whether this resulted in Henri's manipulating his readers by writing in such a way that they could not fail to look up to him. The combination of his spiritual and psychological training would have enabled him to know how to push the right buttons. None of this would necessarily have been conscious, and it is a trap for all writers and journalists. I know myself from experience that if, for example, I am reporting a tragedy or writing about a person's struggle, I am in danger of deliberately selecting words or descriptions that I can guarantee will move people. This can be done ruthlessly by television crews who home in on somebody crying so the coverage makes viewers weep too. Yet even, perhaps especially, for authors of spiritual books, who realize their audience is likely to include sensitive or vulnerable people, there is always the ego-led peril of playing up to the emotions so that readers will think more highly of you than they might otherwise have done.

Like most Catholic priests, Henri might have hoped one day that he would be invited to the Vatican, but he never had the opportunity until the morning he received a notification for an audience with Pope John Paul II. However, he told a papal secretary that he didn't have time because he was too busy at L'Arche. He had, by then, prioritized his life to some extent and knew what the important aspects were. He told a friend toward the end of his life that meeting the pontiff would have gained him nothing but self-esteem, and he didn't need any more of that. In any case, he was sometimes critical of the Roman Catholic hierarchy and the Vatican itself, which he did not agree with. Henri was also offered a post as a bishop but declined because, on the one hand, it would limit the amount of work he could do for religious groups and, on the other, he was keen to remain a universal pastor, with the freedom to travel the globe and speak up for the gospel of peace.

The day before the Gulf War began, Henri joined seven thousand people at the National Episcopal Cathedral in Washington and two thousand more outside on the steps. It was the largest crowd ever to gather there. They then processed with candles to the White House where two thousand more people were waiting. He went with one part of a group but became so engaged speaking to people that he managed to become separated from the main party that was on its way to an all-night vigil in the Metropolitan African Methodist Episcopal Church near the White House where he was due to speak and lead prayers during one of the "hours." Henri couldn't find where he was meant to be going and arrived late, looking somewhat flustered, as though he had been thrown off balance. Becoming detached from the group had panicked him. The event was an unusual context for him because on that occasion all eyes would not be on the well-known writer—some in the African American church had no idea who he was. He also had to tolerate people walking in while he was speaking—not Henri Nouwen groupies but strident Gulf War opponents. "It wasn't a controlled environment where everything was focused on him," Jim Wallis said. "It was much more challenging for a speaker. He wasn't at ease yet even his discomfort indicated his integrity. The fact that he would subject himself to that kind of distress, when he didn't have to, indicated the sincerity of his conviction."

Shortly before the Gulf War ended, Henri arranged to stay with friends for what they had assumed would be a rest, but he persuaded them to put the wheels in motion so that he could give a talk. With little warning, more than eight hundred people in Nashville, Tennessee, came to hear him speak from a heart of mystery and pain. It was surely an indication of Henri's stature in the Christian world that so many assembled at such short notice. That night, Henri entranced them all as he introduced mysticism and loneliness into his two-hour talk, beginning with a time of silence before he prayed:

> Dear God, we are grateful that we are here together and we pray that you let your spirit touch us and to let our heart become more intimately united with your hearts, so that in the midst of a very frightening and dark world we can live a life that is rooted in your love, so deeply rooted that we can live in this world without being destroyed by its dark forces; and let us experience some of the joy and the peace that the world cannot give when it comes from you; and let us trust that that joy and peace will hold us and keep us safe. Amen.

Then he started singing "Spirit of the Living God, fall afresh on me. Melt me, mold me, fill me, use me...." Henri, it should be stated, had a tentative voice that would often begin off-key and grope its way to the right pitch, but he had no self-consciousness about it. He would simply invite people to sing and croak into the song. "It was like a contemplative moment with which he would punctuate his talk but he danced all over the front of the church, had a newsprint stand and drew the timeline image of life," said his former teaching assistant, John Mogabgab, who helped organize the last-minute event. "For two hours people were almost holding their breath. It was amazing to feel the sense of being gathered up by him into something that transcended the moment. It was as if, for those two hours, people were seeing and experiencing something of God's kingdom in their midst."

The guest of honor began by reminding the audience that the United States was a country at war: "The world is in agony. We are a part of it somewhere, whether we like it or not, and it affects our spirit and our deeper life. The life of the Spirit comes into a world that is quite dark and broken. Who am I? I am what I have. I am influenced by what other people say about me. My sense of wellbeing is dependent on the opinions of others. If you believe you are what you have or you are what other people say about you, the world around you has a lot of power. It's not living but surviving." In a voice that raised itself before becoming softer, and could sound excited, then depressed, Henri held the audience's attention as he brought loneliness and holiness into focus through his own performance art:

> God says I am who I am and you are who you are as a child of God....You belong to me. I am yours. You are mine. I have called you from eternity and you are the one who is held safe and embraced in love from eternity to eternity. You belong to me and I am holding you safe. I want you to know that whatever happens to you I am always there, I was always there, I am always there, I will always be there and hold you in my

embrace. You are mine. You are my child. You belong to my home. You belong to my intimate life, and I will never let you go. I will be faithful to you.

Hear it from the heart—the spiritual life starts at the place where you can hear that voice where somehow you can claim that, long before your father, your mother, your sister, your school, your church touched you, loved you, and wounded you, long before that you were held safe in an eternal embrace....I want you to realize that each one of you—and I with you—are people who have been loved, otherwise you wouldn't be here. But each one of you, and myself too, we have all also been hurt and wounded, often precisely by the people who loved us, precisely by the people who are close to us—our father, our mother, our sisters, our brothers, our teachers, our school, our church.

Then Henri lowered his voice and, clearly reflecting on his recent past, spoke as though he were about to make a private confession to the entire audience:

If I think about myself as a nervous person who has a lot of worries and anxieties about what to do with my life, I am needy, and I am lonely.... I have all these emotions—I'm lonely, anxious, fearful, and I'm a trembling person. Then [I meet] somebody else like me. I might get very attracted to that person. We'd be very compatible. And I'm lonely. You're lonely. Why don't we get together? I'm wounded, you're wounded, maybe we can heal each other? Get closer. Get closer. Get closer and then your fingers interlock and you say "I have been with you for so long and I'm still lonely. Maybe we should take some distance. There is a lot of pain there in the relationship. A lot of breakages. And we've suffered a lot. I've suffered immensely from my own loneliness and from my hope that some other person could finally take it away. I'm still doing it—he, she....

Then the tone grew in stature as the preacher man moved on:

The vision that Jesus gives us is this: that I am unconditionally loved. I belong to God and I am a person who can trust that. When I need another person who also is rooted in the heart of God, then the Spirit of God in me can recognize the Spirit of God in the other person, and we can start building a new space, a new home, a house, a community....God has given me a heart that yearns to be loved, so intimately that only the one who has given me that heart can give me that love. It's only there in God that I can basically trust that I am well held. But that same love sets me free to enter community with other people, even when that community is a very limited one and is not the total communion that my heart desires. Only when I live in communion with God can I live in community that is not perfect, and kind of love the other person and create a space in which we might be quite distant or very close, but we can still allow something new to be born—a child, friendship, joy, community, strangers. The space we can create precisely because we are all rooted in the same heart that loves us. That is the mystery of the spiritual life. It starts precisely there in the heart, and then we can live in the community.

It is evident that Henri was still wrestling with issues of love, intimacy, and belonging and, as with his writing, he was not reluctant to share some of his emotional struggles with the audience. While this could be considered open and honest, it might also have been another indication of the loneliness and insecurity that could besiege him. In his later years, Henri preached about "Being the Beloved" with such vigor, people might have wondered if he were almost trying to convince himself. The spirituality brought consolation to many, but during a discussion about it on a retreat I was giving, one member of the group, Mary Garcia, reflected on the people she tried to help in her life and how they experienced "belovedness" themselves.

Mary is a psychodynamic counselor with The Marie Trust, a service within a homelessness center in Glasgow, Scotland. With two colleagues, she works on a long-term basis with clients trying to help them make sense of who they are and the difficulties encountered in their lives. Up to a hundred people a day come through their doors. Some sleep rough but most live in temporary accommodation. As a way of coping, many are burdened by drug and alcohol addictions, now officially classed as "multiple complex trauma."

Mary works with women, some of whom are in the process of leaving prostitution. She made the point that Nouwen was passionate about how much God loved people and delighted in who they were. His life and writings exuded a growing awareness of his being "loved into life." Yet every day, Mary told us, she met "those among us for whom this experience is so alien, impossible to imagine, and so out of reach—babies born into the world who were conceived through rape and sexual abuse; those born into the world who later experience only abuse by the parents whom they so longed could love and care for them. They are wrapped in messages of their own worthlessness, sitting in the sure belief that there is something wrong with them and that they are therefore completely unlovable. Their pain and shame are so deep that they cannot look up for fear others might recognize that in them, and with that comes the expectation of another rejection." We sat in silence as Mary powerfully asked, "How do you offer care and love to those who cannot look at you, who plead for the very love they cannot accept because to take such a risk may cause even more hurt and rejection?"

In the summer of 1992, during one of Henri's trips abroad, I heard him preach on belovedness at a Christian Arts Festival in England. I arranged to rendezvous with him at the Northampton Moat House; a more unlikely location to meet my spiritual hero is difficult to imagine. Known to be one of the most restless figures in the world of contemporary spirituality, Henri was so restless that day that he began to leave our agreed rendezvous before I had even arrived. The interview had been arranged for noon and, arriving early in the hotel car park, I had used the spare time to sharpen my questions. Before noon, I headed into the entrance hall and was about to ask the receptionist to call Henri's room when I spied a tall, bespectacled man in a blue-check flat cap, scarf, dark raincoat, grey trousers, and bright red shoulder bag hovering in the lobby. It had to be him. He was with his genial assistant, filmmaker Bart Gavigan.

Although Henri looked different from how I had imagined him, I confidently introduced myself. He smiled, and we shook hands. "We thought you weren't coming," he said. I decided not to be too defensive by insisting that I was, in fact, completely on time; before long we were ascending in an elevator, saying little, and heading to Bart's room. Common territory for both itinerant preachers and wandering journalists, hotels are not the best environments for recording radio interviews, but sitting in front of the portable television, we began to record, the gesticulating arms clouting the microphone from time to time.

The interview covered various aspects of the pastor's life: his new book, *The Return of the Prodigal Son*, and how he had come to write it; his spirituality about making prints from negatives; his life at L'Arche; and his search for God. For some reason, I ended by asking him if he had a wild side. He laughed, "That's what I'm doing with you now. I'm being wound up and down at the same time." I brought in the mystical, speaking figuratively of the dark night of the soul and Mount Carmel. It led him to recall a visit to the Holy Land when he had climbed Mount Tabor: "I didn't take the normal route. I climbed right through the bushes and I got totally exhausted, sick, and miserable because it was just an awful trip to get there. I got lost and all that. But when I finally came to the top and looked over, I suddenly saw something that I wouldn't have seen if I had taken the bus up because somehow my whole body was seeing it."

After the conversation, Henri and Bart needed to head off to the Greenbelt Festival at Castle Ashby some miles away, so I offered to drive them. Henri sat beside me in the front seat. After the animated interview, I noticed that he seemed quieter, almost preoccupied. According to my journal, "We chatted about his life and mine." Then, out of the blue, he announced, "I'm an ambitious person." I wasn't expecting to hear that and wondered if he sensed that I, like many others, was putting him on a pedestal a little, something of course he did not care for. I asked him for his influences. "I don't have any. I like art and conversations." Once again, it was an answer that surprised me. During lunch, which had a eucharistic quality about it, I sat next to Henri. I remember how we all held hands around the table and prayed. I noticed that, just before presenting his seminar, Henri seemed anxious about what he was going to say, but what emerged from his lips on belovedness that day was sensational. When it was time for me to leave Greenbelt, Henri made a point of coming up and, with great sincerity, thanked me for staying to listen to him. He told me to keep in touch, which I did. I distinctly remember how sad he seemed to say farewell. I think we both felt connected with each other. We shook hands and I walked across to the tent exit. As I was about to head to my car, I glanced back. Henri was still looking, uncharacteristically, I later learned, as he was always rushing off. But that afternoon he stood and waved, and I waved back. It was a poignant moment for both of us.

9

THE HOLY MAN

May each minute carry me further into the depths of your mystery.

—Elizabeth of the Trinity

It was something of a revelation and a reassurance for me to learn directly from the lips of Henri Nouwen that he was not a particularly harmonious person who held his spiritual life in equilibrium. It wasn't about seeking a balance but about maintaining a tension, he said. Henri lived what he had to live as intensely as he could at any moment he was asked to live it. "I'm not trying to be a harmonious person. I'm trying to be somebody who lives faithfully, works hard and prays deeply, and trusts that God will be there with me." Praying never came easy for the priest who guided so many people into a deeper relationship with God. He could get fidgety, distracted, and look at his watch. Or there could be a fervid zeal about his posture that people did not fail to notice. A nun who prayed with him prostrate remembered the intensity in his voice as he begged God to protect his friends in South America. "I opened my eyes and saw his massive hands tensed with the depths of his words, dug deeply into the carpet," she wrote on a website. Once, a lay assistant at L'Arche in Trosly walked calmly into an oratory and suddenly caught sight of a huge, long body in full-length prostration in front of the Blessed Sacrament. She said she had an overwhelming awareness that the priest was in the presence of God and that God was with him.

For Henri, prayer involved the body in many different postures. Sometimes he was too tired to concentrate as he felt he should, so his physical position got him into the proper frame of mind. Prayer was first and foremost listening to God and being open to the Divine Voice that was always speaking. It was bringing into the presence of God all that you were, including negative feelings toward another person. God could handle anything, he believed, but it was always important to convert thoughts into prayer. The difference between unceasing thinking and unceasing prayer was that prayer was thinking in dialogue. It was a move from self-centered monologue to a divine conversation with God. Henri always felt connected with Jesus. If he were preaching at a Sunday Mass, he wouldn't be burning the midnight oil on a homily. Only after breakfast would he open the Gospel, assimilate it in ten minutes, and be ready to preach passionately and articulately. This would never have been possible had he not been a man with a disciplined prayer life. I gained a sense of his scrupulous self-control in his archives at Yale, where I came across a spiral-bound notebook with immaculate handwriting. This was an intimate, spiritual journal of one of Henri's thirty-day Ignatian retreats, in which he recorded his thoughts in English, Dutch, and French (perhaps to protect confidentiality as much as possible). Written during his year at Trosly, it reveals the inner life of a holy man who dialogues with God but, like many of us, finds it difficult to let God be at the center and to trust that God's love is sufficient. As he reflects on the passion, he is grateful for new insights he has received into the Eucharist and to Mary for her protection. He is repentant for his sins and resolves, in future, to keep calm and to live more readily in an ongoing spirit of prayer. His meditations on the way of the cross and the death of Jesus are moving and intimate, yet no different from the way he writes in his books. While the "confidential" on the front of the book was lifted and I was told I could draw from it for my research, there is such a confessional tone about this sacred document that it seems inappropriate to be too specific, but if more evidence were ever needed that Henri was on a mystical journey, this is it. He even notes that a prayer he offers to St. Thérèse of Lisieux brings him much consolation.

Wherever he pitched his tent, Henri had an innate capacity to create a sacred space into which he would then invite others. In Washington, DC, the Church of the Saviour's Servant Leadership School offered him the use of a top-floor apartment where he would take his time to rearrange the furniture and create for himself the equivalent of a small altar, draping over a chair or small dressing table, sheets, towels, or whatever linen was available. He would then look for an icon and cross, placing them together by the holy table. This became a private place he could use for prayer and worship, but he did not always like to praise God on his own. There were a few "privileged occasions" when Diana Chambers would drop him off at the apartment late at night and he would invite her into the newly created liturgical space and light a candle so they could say Night Prayer together. Through that example of faithfulness, Henri taught Diana a sense of discipline: that all Christian people are responsible for this dimension of their relationship with Jesus and the need to do it respectfully.

The inclusive service of compline would last twenty minutes. "His form of prayer was always simple and inviting, so I loved and cherished those times of praying with him in a very private way," Diana told me. "We always had a time of open and spontaneous prayer which we would just formulate ourselves so there was always plenty of time to bring into that space the concerns we were personally carrying. I remember that he always used to reflect on the scriptures. He would read the passage and immediately say how it was speaking to him and what he wanted to share. It was precious." It was obvious to Diana that Henri had a personal place of holiness within himself—and the Christian mystic himself was only too conscious that a sacred space without could also speak to a sacred space within.

As a rule, he found it easier to pray in places where people had prayed for centuries, and harder to pray in places where a prayer might never have been uttered. In an empty train compartment, a hotel room, or even a quiet study, he sometimes detected a spirit that held him back from prayer. Henri was always grateful for the friends who prayed for him, especially when he felt frightened. He also had a closeness to certain saints or holy people in the Church's memory. They spoke to him of faithful witness and strength, and sometimes guided him in his hour of need. "In times of struggle, I do not hesitate to ask them to pray for me, as they encourage me to practice discernment and live a spiritual life," he writes.[1] Whether still living or with the "great cloud of witnesses," true saints were accessible and available to help us. They are often men and women with ordinary lives and ordinary problems but who hold a clear and unwavering focus on God and God's people. For Henri, belonging to the communion of saints meant being with all people transformed by the Spirit of Jesus. It fascinated him how some saints or holy people never really leave us when they die. Their deaths somehow free them from the constraints of earthly existence and bring them nearer to more people than they could ever have known when they were alive. Henri followed the advice of St. Teresa of Avila to focus on the goodness of God in times of discernment. He said that it helped him fight the demons of despair, self-rejection, and fear, overcoming the powers of darkness with the power of God. He often repeated St. Teresa's prayer *Solo Dios basta* (God alone is enough) when he needed to discern what he was hearing and experiencing was of God or not.[2] Henri also found strength in the words of St. Teresa's spiritual friend,

St. John of the Cross, who writes of a light too bright for the eyes to see in the midst of darkness, vulnerability, and fear.

When Henri invited his friend Jim Forest to stay with him at his father's house in Holland, he told him that an elderly priest, who had translated the writings of St. John of the Cross and St. Teresa of Avila, lived in a nearby village. Henri admired the translations but also had "a tremendous feeling" about this priest's gift for hearing confessions, so he arranged to go to make his own. "When he came out, I could see in his face, not only the relief and joy that one does feel after going to confession, but also some distress," Jim Forest said. "That was connected to the fact that he was the first person in seven years to go to the priest for confession. He had never heard anybody's confession for seven years. When Henri approached him, the priest looked disbelievingly at him. 'You really want me to hear your confession?' Any priest can hear confession, but some have a great gift for it. Here was someone with a rare gift, a charism for helping people experience the mercy of God but nobody wanted it. At a time when nobody was going to confession, Henri was. There was a strange sense of exile in that. In the Netherlands, confessionals were being used as closets for storing unwanted furniture and boxes. It was all right to ask about making your confession, but it wasn't a common practice on a Saturday night any longer."

As you can imagine, Henri was himself an understanding confessor. "I'll never forget it," Brother Christian told me at the Abbey of the Genesee. "His voice was low, and he spoke of my failings. Boy! I walked out of there and felt it had been really something. One of the greatest times I ever made use of the sacrament of penance was with Henri Nouwen. It was a beautiful experience. He took about forty-five minutes and had the ability to put me at rest. It wasn't an easy forty-five minutes. He didn't do a lot of talking, neither did I. He just brought up the limitations and failings I mentioned. As monks, we go to confession hopefully about once a month so our slate by the mercy of God is pretty well clean.

That was Holy Saturday before the big day of the year. That was a tremendous experience. And when he celebrated the Mass, there was no one else around—just him and Jesus."

A primary interest for Henri was always his own healing and everybody else's. He was constantly aware of the wounds in people—his own wounds as well, of course, but not only them. Jim Forest recalled, "When my former wife left me and I was living through a period of extreme depression, Henri would call from Yale every month at least—maybe every couple of weeks, as though he were calling from the neighboring town. He simply wanted to see how I was doing. Nobody else did that. It was something quite remarkable about Henri—knowing when somebody was suffering and being able to show how much he cared. At a certain point, he called and asked why I didn't come to America and stay with him for a while. I said I would love to but could not afford it. Henri said that he would arrange for his travel agent to send the ticket. So I went and we celebrated Easter together. After being with him for some days, he suggested it might be helpful if I went up to stay at the Abbey of the Genesee, and he arranged that. This kind of extraordinary caring for another person was something unusual. I could just go for walks, or bicycle rides, or listen to music. I couldn't write very much. I was more than half-dead. Reading was too much for me. It was total numbness. One of the best things that happened during that period was going and staying with Henri. It was very inspiring. There was this contagious enthusiasm that you could not be untouched by, no matter how you were feeling."

Whatever mental anguish he was going through himself, when people really needed Henri, he was still able to be totally present to them. Louis Dupré, a professor of the philosophy of religion at Yale, suffered a serious depression during his initial years there. His first wife had left him. "I was just lost," he told me. "Through his help, I was able in my own strange way to sublimate this spiritually to a great extent. Henri's guidance was purely spiritual but with a great deal of psychological insight. He didn't make any silly spiritual statements—anything he said he could psycho-logically justify. It was quite amazing. In the process, I realized how deeply emotional states and frailties could be related to the spiritual. He did me an enormous amount of good. He observed none of the rules of Freudian analysis. He wanted me to speak, then he would say something. Sometimes he would ask questions, then he would become very firm, perhaps too firm, in what he thought was true. But he could get away with it because he had an enormously open spirituality, maybe because of his psychological background, but more, I think, as a result of his private convictions.

"He was able to speak to modern people in the world with modern problems such as anxiety and family disruption. That was his real power. He was not in any school at all. It grew out of his development. There was a serenity about it, but he felt he had to work things out. Everything he did—the greatness of Henri and also the smallness of the man—was his own. In all things, he wanted to be free. He only overcame the tensions and problems in his own life by being totally spiritual. I don't think he had much of a choice. It was either that or he would have gone down completely."

The Belgian professor, who taught courses on mysticism at Yale and has written extensively on the subject, hesitated when I asked him if he considered Henri a mystic. "That word I would use lightly because it has so many meanings," he said. "If by mystic you mean someone who was gifted with extraordinary graces—and that unhappily is the modern meaning of the word—I would say he was not. But Henri was deeply spiritual, so if we mean mystic in that ancient sense, then he definitely was—no doubt about it. The authenticity of his spirituality was evident to me. The guy was absolutely sincere—brutally with himself and others."

It was Henri's gift of lifting the burdens that others were carry-ing that not only endeared him to so many people but also revealed his own personal holiness. He had a wisdom around listening, not becoming entangled in the problem but rather staying with the per-son. He helped immensely not by necessarily solving the issue but giving the person a direction that they recognized as the one they should follow. At Daybreak, he was the spiritual accompanier of Lorenzo Sforza-Cesarini, an assistant who came from an aristocratic landowning family in Italy. "I was looking for direction and once I got to know Henri, I felt quite connected with him," he said. "He called me to be a spiritual person. When I came with my problems, he would always have to turn things around and help me see there was something more beautiful, beyond what I saw everyday as dark. He would always call me to that. He really felt my pain, and this connected me with him. Eventually it became a reciprocal friendship. He was a very strong advocate for standing up and claiming your life. His charisma was probably second to none. He wanted to plant things in people and really hold you. I loved his spirit and enthusiasm for life. He gave me the joy of life."

Once, a distraught friend told Henri how her baby niece had drowned in a swimming pool in California. Understandably, she was unable to forget the tragedy, but after sharing it with Henri, she found herself being able to think more clearly. Years later, she reminded him of the pastoral care she had received from him at the time, but he had no recollection of what he had said or any realization of how his presence had consoled her. He hadn't said anything that the friend could remember specifically. "It was just the way he had been."

That was the effect he had on people—continually.

Henri's mystical presence also flowed through the Eucharist, the center of his daily life. He would celebrate Mass wherever he was—a friend's house, his father's living room, or an uninspiring hotel room. Anyone was welcome. His Masses at Yale were legendary. Louis Dupré remembered one of his "beautiful" Masses in that chapel where all kinds of people were present. On that occasion, Henri explained that, the following week, he would not be present so instead an Anglican priest would celebrate Mass. "He was never involved in the polemics in the church because he didn't think them important. His whole attitude was very traditional but at the

same time he didn't feel tied by it. Spiritually, he was a free man."
Henri celebrated informally in a way that honored the spirit of the
Church of which he was a part. He never aimed to embarrass his
Church, which is why he would never do anything publicly that
was inappropriate for him as a priest but would quietly find his
own way. He was never trying to make a point but always a priest
yearning for people to be fed by the Body and Blood of Christ, and
to be drawn into that mystical relationship through eucharistic
participation.

For the Eucharist in the Dayspring Chapel of the L'Arche
community in Ontario, Henri used (in place of traditional chalices) several large cups made by a glassblower through which the
consecrated wine could be seen. For him, they spoke of a new way
of being priest and a new way of being human. He sat behind a
low table in a circle of men and women with intellectual disabilities and the carers. Although Henri was the Catholic chaplain at
L'Arche, it was an ecumenical community, and while firmly rooted
in his own tradition, he was always open-minded. In 1989, when
Barbara Harris became the first woman to be ordained a bishop
in the Anglican Communion, he told the community he had no
problem with the historic decision at all, but most importantly, he
pointed out, Barbara Harris fasted every Friday.

The Rev. Wendy Lywood, a house assistant living in one of
the homes and involved also in the pastoral life of the community,
said that what had moved her about him—and what was "his gift
to the world"—was Henri's wonderful way of interpreting the gospel. When his secretary Connie Ellis was dying, Henri was away
in Germany writing, but he came back to be with her. At the hospital, she was unable to talk very much, so Henri read to her the
Gospel for the day—Jesus in the Synagogue at Nazareth quoting the
Prophet Isaiah. He spoke gently to her, "You know, Connie, you're
poor right now but I've come to tell you good news. You're blind
right now because you don't see what lies ahead of you after death,
but I have come to tell you that you are going to see something

that will be beyond all your imagining." Henri went through every phrase, using it in a pastoral but powerful way to talk to Connie about her dying, what that would be like, and how that Gospel had relevance as she lay dying. "It was one of the most moving times I ever spent with Henri just because of his passion," Wendy recalled. "He was saying, 'This is the truth of the Gospel, Connie, and I am coming to proclaim that to you as your friend and as a priest and as a pastor.' It was beautiful."

THE ART OF GAZING

Two years after Ukraine gained its independence from the Soviet Union in the aftermath of its dissolution at the end of the Cold War, Henri packed a few clothes and was off again—this time, a little apprehensively because of tensions in the country. Eastern Orthodoxy had strongly influenced the architecture, literature, and music of Ukraine. Outside a small wooden chapel in the bleak suburbs of Lviv, on his first evening there, Henri heard the singing of a chant, *Hospody pomyluy*, Russian words meaning "Lord have mercy," which featured among the Taizé chants he appreciated. He felt reassured and connected as he listened. For Orthodox Christians, the words form the heart of the Jesus Prayer that lies at the core of Eastern liturgy. Nouwen journaled that "Lord have mercy" was the prayer of God's people, one that had resounded through centuries of struggle, wars, persecution, and oppression. While they were words of the liturgy, they also belonged to the intimate prayer of the heart. Henri spoke them often without being aware of it—when he was falling asleep, going out for a stroll, driving his car, or waiting for a friend to arrive. His private spiritual life was not without its ups and downs, but the prayer "Lord Jesus Christ, have mercy on me" remained in the shadows, even during his driest periods.[3]

Henri's lifelong love of liturgy was profoundly influenced by the Christian East. While he lived and worshipped in the West, nurtured every day by the Latin-rite Eucharist, his occasional contact with the Liturgy of St. John Chrysostom enabled him to understand what it meant to be in the world without being of it. Participating in Eastern liturgies gave him a sense of being in heaven before leaving earth. During his pilgrimage to the Ukraine, visiting children with developmental disabilities, it gradually dawned on him that his love of prayer, the liturgical life, and sacred art, especially icons, had all been greatly nurtured by the Christian East. He recalled the influence of *The Way of a Pilgrim*, the eighteenth-century story of a peasant who walked through the countryside visiting holy places in Ukraine and simply repeating the words "Lord Jesus Christ, have mercy on me." This prayer traveled from his lips to his heart until it became one with his breathing. Henri felt the book gave charming and even humorous expression to the Orthodox tradition of the prayer of the heart, also known as *hesychasm* (from the Greek *hesychazein*, which means "to rest.").[4]

The main writings of the Hesychastic movement, which Henri believed were mystical, are found in the *Philokalia*, a collection of texts written between the fourth and fifteenth centuries by spiritual masters of the Orthodox Christian tradition and regarded as second only to the Bible in terms of influence in the recent history of the Orthodox Church. These were helpful when Henri came to write about the solitude, silence, and prayer of the Egyptian desert fathers and mothers in his classic *The Way of the Heart*.[5] A monk later put together excerpts from the *Philokalia*, which were eventually translated into English and published as *The Art of Prayer*.[6] Few books on prayer made such a lasting impression on Henri. Much of it is devoted to the writings of the Russian Orthodox monk and priest Theophan the Recluse (1815–94), whom Henri often quoted.

"I really believe that part of what drew him to Orthodoxy was the idea of an alternative approach to Christianity in which you could have at once a deep sense of freedom and at the same time a deep sense of fidelity to tradition—both appealed to him greatly," Father John Garvey, an Orthodox priest, said over lunch in New York. "He understood that they do not need to be contradictory, and he found something of that in Orthodoxy. In Holland, the Church had become very secular; there was a great falling away. Many people stopped having anything to do with the Church including some people in his own family. The politicization of Christianity was also happening, a struggle between the forces of the left and the forces of the right, as though that were all it was about. Henri found all of that discouraging, and then he looked at the clarity of the desert fathers or the fathers of the Church and saw an alternative that appealed to him.

"The attraction to contemplative life was extremely important to him. I think he saw in the stillness in icons and the way they could become the focus of an interior stillness something profoundly helpful to prayer. His book on icons continues to appeal to a lot of people. He had a lot of Orthodox fans. I know a woman who, before his death, wanted to get him to talk at our church, St. Vladimir's, and after his death wanted to get together and talk of how much his books meant to her."

At first, Henri found the sacred images rather inhospitable, but as he began to pray before them, they gradually revealed their secrets to him, leading him far beyond his daily preoccupations and into the kingdom of God. They were indeed "windows into the eternal." After studying their history and meaning, he produced *Behold the Beauty of the Lord*,[7] a beautiful series of meditations on four Russian icons that, for him, express different aspects of the mystery of salvation and are intimately connected with the experience of love: the icon of the *Holy Trinity* invites us to dwell in the house of love; the icon of the *Virgin of Vladimir* assures us that we belong to God; the icon of the *Saviour of Zvenigorod* unveils the face of the Lord, and the icon of the *Descent of the Holy Spirit* commissions us to liberate the world. With the beguiling charm of a spiritual master, he invites his readers to gaze at the icons attentively and pray with them. He believed they had been created "for the sole purpose of offering access, through the gate of the visible, to the mystery of the invisible," leading us "into the inner room of prayer" and bringing us "close to the heart of God."[8] For Henri, the icons speak especially to the heart that searches for God. In their own unique language, they draw him into closer communion with the God who loves. For Henri, they were always invitations to divine intimacy.

Jim and Nancy Forest remembered him arriving in Holland with a reproduction of the icon of the *Holy Trinity* as a wedding gift. "He came up from Paris and was awfully excited that he'd found this little shop where there were very good reproductions of icons," Jim recalled. "He was so pleased at the quality. I still remember sitting with him at a coffee bar at Schiphol airport very carefully going through every detail of the icon and his joy about what he was able to find in it. He did have a spectacular gift for seeing and being able to describe the significance of the symbols. He couldn't have made it more clear how important icons were to him."

Art helped Henri get in touch with the transcendent, and, not only did it slow him down, it brought him to a halt— sometimes for hours or even days. When he visited an art gallery, he might rush on ahead, up the stairs and onto the right floor. But once he had located his treasure, he would appear to stare with immense concentration—oblivious of his surroundings. What he was really doing was walking around inside the painting, seeing it from within.

Henri's close affinity with the work and life of van Gogh brought him under the radar of a mystic from the artistic world. It could be said that Henri is the van Gogh of spiritual writers, except that his sales of seven million books could hardly compare to the artist's two sold paintings in his lifetime. The turbulent emotional lives of both men mirrored each other in many ways. Few people influenced him more than van Gogh, whose deep wounds and immense gifts brought him in touch with his own brokenness and talents in a unique manner. He was restored and renewed by the endless hours he spent looking at paintings in a museum in the Netherlands and carefully studying Vincent's letters to his brother Theo. In times of solitude, he heard a voice he felt he could listen to and make connections between van Gogh's struggle and his own. The mystic in van Gogh guided the mystic in Henri, who claimed the former as his own wounded healer. More than any of his other courses, seminars on *The Ministry of Vincent van Gogh* at Yale Divinity School had a much more profound effect on students who were never more personally, intellectually, or emotionally involved than when they were attentively looking at van Gogh's drawings and paintings. They spent long hours in silence gazing at slides. There was no need for the tutor to try to explain or analyze. Henri wanted his students to have a direct experience of the ecstasy and the agony of the painter and his search for meaning. The artist seemed to touch them in places that no writer had managed to penetrate. The letters expressed a longing for a God who was tangible and alive, who could comfort and console, and who cared for the poor and people who suffered. To Henri, the God of van Gogh seemed real and direct, visible in nature and in people, especially the compassionate, weak, and vulnerable.

As I read through his carefully planned teaching notes, it was apparent how dedicated Henri had been to his subject, a contemplative teacher helping young people to see God in new ways. I came across one paper in which he introduces the course to future ministers: "In this seminar, the life and works of Vincent van Gogh will be the main source from which to raise questions about the nature of Christian ministry. The intensity of Vincent's struggles, as well as the powerful way in which he expressed these struggles in paintings and letters, offer a unique 'case' for pastoral theological reflection."

Chris Glaser, who attended the seminars, sensed psychological connections between his tutor and the painter: "I believe that Henri was drawn to van Gogh because they shared a profound sense of loneliness," he told me. "Loneliness is the wilderness for the writer, the artist, and the contemplative. Writing, creativity, and prayer are not ways out of the wilderness, but a way to make the wilderness blossom, to turn the ache of feeling lonely to a fulfilling solitude, transforming 'lone' to 'alone,' which is derived from joining the words 'all-one.' Both Vincent and Henri were passionately reaching out to others through their work: Vincent in his paintings and Henri in his books. They were intense in their personal relationships as well. In their loneliness, I believe both were driven by *eros*, that urge in us to find union with another or with God. What fuels the lover fuels the artist, writer, and mystic as well."

There are references to art in many of Henri Nouwen's books, always written up in an engaging manner and often associated with an expedition he has made. For example, in *Letters to Marc about Jesus*, he recounts a visit to the Isenheim Altarpiece near Colmar, France. A multiple series of panels, it was painted between 1513 and 1515 for the chapel at a hospital for victims of the plague. According to most authorities, Matthias Grünewald was the creator of this masterpiece. Henri's descriptions of the panels are vivid enough, but his spiritual responses to what he observes are even more compelling. He explains that he remained at the altar for more than three hours, learning more about suffering and resurrection than any amount of reading would have taught him. Grünewald's crucified and risen Christ became so ingrained in Henri's memory and imagination that wherever he went or stayed, he was able to call the artist to mind and knew he must remain united to Jesus.[9] By entering into the picture, then, Henri received something of a mystical insight into the fulfillment of his vocation. He entered the mind, not only of the painter, but also the patients who would have originally reflected on the panels and understood that God was with them in their trials. Grünewald was showing them what the Eucharist really gave them. Incorporated into the suffering of Jesus, they could trust that they would also share in his resurrection. Henri's immersion in the pictures yields a deeper spiritual awareness of his own calling. In also sharing what he has experienced with his readers, they, too, are encouraged to "go within" and experience the transcendent power of art.

However, it was Rembrandt's *The Return of the Prodigal Son* that spoke to him as art had never done. When he first saw a poster copy, he felt something stirring powerfully within and he envisioned what he most yearned for—a homecoming, an experience of belonging, a moment of safety, an embrace of love. Perhaps he thought back to his early childhood and his questions from the playpen. "This is what I most desire," he said to himself as he looked at the poster, "to be welcomed home so fully and so intimately." Later, when he spent several days in St. Petersburg, sitting in front of the masterpiece, examining its every detail, he had a further revelation—while the younger son is being embraced by the father, the elder son is observing events at a distance. Was he also like him—still angry, jealous, resentful? Perhaps he was remembering how his father placed expectations on him and not on his siblings, and how embittered he became. It was only after the breakdown at L'Arche that he grew into an awareness that he was, in fact, called to be the father of the community. "It really hit me as a very new call that I was finally called to succeed the father in a sense, to become the father, and to receive others home, and to make my own suffering and my own struggle a way of becoming ready to receive others home," he told me. "The painting became the summary of my whole life but also a call for me to become something new."

But was there a danger, I wondered, that he was merely projecting his own needs onto the painting and hoping it would reflect what he wanted to see. "I don't think it's a danger," he responded swiftly. "I think indeed a painting *allows* me to project a lot of things there, to come in touch with things in myself. I am not suggesting that Rembrandt expected anybody to use the painting the way I did. But I have that wonderful freedom to look at a painting and to let the painting become an icon that brings me in touch with my deepest self. The painting did have that enormous power to say something about *me*. Indeed, I projected into the painting a lot of my own struggles. But I was rewarded for that projection by coming to know myself better. I was looking at the painting from the perspective of a human being who lives a lot of pain and a lot of joy, and has a lot of yearnings, and wants to be able to come in touch with that." Laughing, the writer added, "It's also true that, once I got in touch with the painting, I couldn't *not* speak about it. But it was very personal."

Henri had a lifelong attraction to the arts—a fascination that could border on the obsessive. One New Year's Eve found him perching near the front of a concert hall as he settled into a program of uplifting Viennese waltzes. As the orchestra struck up, he moved his body closer so that he was almost drooping over the edge of the little balcony, getting as close as he could to the conductor who was moving his arms with alluring aplomb. The entire process of creativity excited him. With that boy-like wonder of his, he sat engrossed in the performance, never letting his eyes divert from the frock-coated maestro and the acrobatic routines of his slim baton. Perhaps he saw in that energetic figure a mirror image of himself, for anyone who ever watched "the whole vibrating system of Henri" spring into action would not be slow in comparing his style to the way an animated conductor brings alive the Berlin Philharmonic.

An accomplished pianist, Henri was fine-tuned to many forms of classical music, including complex compositions from the hand of Bach. When a Dutch friend found him listening to a Mozart piano concerto, Henri explained that he was "discovering it." As he imagined the conductor at work, he came to understand the way in which God supports people in their lives. This was a mystic's perception. When writing in one of his books about the "global ecstasy" of a new international order—the movement from fear to love—he draws on his musical sensitivity to make a spiritual point. Dreaming great dreams is like composing a new symphony that, once created, becomes familiar. Beethoven's Fifth

Symphony now sounds as if it always existed, he points out. It has become so familiar, we can hardly believe there was ever a time without it and that each movement had to be conceived, note by note, by a human being. "It was not written in the stars, it had to be made. So too, new ways must be found for nations to lift up their unity in global celebration, and praise the Creator in ecstatic, joyful song."[10]

Leonard Bernstein became his "most revered music teacher," and a scene from his *Mass*—a musical in memory of John F. Kennedy—embodied Henri's theological concept of putting brokenness under the blessing and revealed to him the mystery of his life. Toward the end of the work, the priest is lifted up by his people, towering high above the admiring crowd and carrying in his hand a glass chalice. Suddenly, the human pyramid collapses and the priest tumbles down. His vestments are torn off, the chalice falls to the ground and is shattered. As the priest walks barefoot through the debris of his former glory (wearing only blue jeans and a T-shirt), children's voices are heard singing, "*Laude, laude, laude.*" Immediately, the priest spies the broken chalice. He stares at it for a long time before remarking, "I never realized that broken glass could shine so brightly."[11]

That theatrical moment was surely symbolic of Henri's own life and ministry.

10

REVELATIONS OF DIVINE LOVE

We are more truly in heaven than on earth.

—Julian of Norwich

It was during his ten years at L'Arche that Henri Nouwen came as close as he had ever come to physical death. While trying to hitchhike on an icy winter's morning in Richmond Hill, he was struck by the outside rearview mirror of a van and had to undergo immediate surgery for the removal of his spleen at a hospital in Toronto. Henri had always said that it was the interruptions of his everyday life that most revealed to him the divine mystery of which he was part—and lying on a bed in an emergency room, while losing blood, proved no exception. In a subsequent paperback, *Beyond the Mirror*,[1] he wrote that his accident brought him to the portal of death and a new experience of God. Perhaps only a genuine mystic could have seen it that way. The prospect of death was all too real, but on this occasion, Henri, normally no stranger to despair, did not feel anguished. The simple fact that he was treated with so much dignity and respect by strangers made him feel safe. Far from wanting to flee from the situation in fright, Henri experienced deep belonging and even at-homeness. "I do not have many conscious memories of being so completely cared for and, at the same time, of being taken so seriously. Perhaps it was this that filled me with such a profound sense of security."[2]

Henri summoned the courage to prepare himself and his friends for the possibility that he might die. He writes that he let himself "enter into a place I had never been before: the portal of death. I wanted to know that place, to 'walk around' it, and make myself ready for a life beyond life."[3] Then, for the first time in his life, he says that he experienced pure and unconditional love, an intensely personal presence that asked him to trust. "It was not a warm light, a rainbow, or an open door that I *saw* but a human yet divine presence that I *felt*, inviting me to come closer and to let go of all fears."[4]

The essential struggle was not about departing from loved ones but about leaving behind people he had not forgiven or who had not forgiven him. He was clearly in a liminal state. Although he recovered, he felt he should remain "on the other side" while being sent back to this world to live eternity while exploring the human search in time. Having touched eternity, it was impossible to point toward it as though it were not already here. Jesus had spoken from his intimate, unbreakable communion with the Father into the world and thereby connected heaven with earth. Henri, who had difficulty sleeping after the accident, would spend the rest of his life with this sense of speaking from eternity into time, a theologian looking at the world from God's perspective. But a few years later, he found himself in hospital again—this time with a dangerous infection and another brush with death. All that he had learned through life and experienced through his encounters with the nearness of dying taught him that death was like a second birth, leading him to a new way of living: He had nothing to say about his first birth but felt he had much to say about his second birth—and he wanted to prepare for it.

For a deeper insight into this period of Henri's life, I spoke to Professor Michael Christensen, who was one of his students. Michael has coauthored (with his wife, Professor Rebecca Laird) several bestselling books about Nouwen's spirituality. "After his accident, Henri didn't seem to care as much about academic respectability or systematic thought but began to speak 'from eternity into time,' which was a prophetic state of mind and heart," he said. "Looking at his most mystical works, this new mission fulfilled a life-long quest, a deeper need and longing for a transcendent spirituality—a timeless realm where there is unconditional love and acceptance.

"When Henri speaks on the traditional spiritual life and disciplines, only the classically initiated can access them. When he speaks psychologically, he's time-bound and ordinary. But when he speaks prophetically, his spirit is accessible and those who are mystically inclined—regardless of their denomination or religion—sense that he speaks from a place of depth that has universal significance.

"Henri has more in common with Thomas Merton, Meister Eckhart, Hildegard of Bingen, Julian of Norwich, and St. John of the Cross (all of whom he liked) than other ordinary Catholic writers. I believe Henri will be compared favorably with these great people who spoke from the heart—mystically and prophetically—in a way that was not commonly understood by those around him in his own tradition. This charism will help preserve his legacy."

FLYING AND CATCHING

Growing up in Europe, where circuses often arrived in town, Henri was used to going to the big top from a young age. The mystery of circus life had long intrigued and enthralled him. His one-time teaching assistant, John Mogabgab, wondered if Henri might have seen himself as a sad clown. He perceived himself to be needy and fretful, outwardly at home but not feeling at home, loved but not feeling loved, needed but not feeling needed. This was all part of the agony. As a performer himself, though, Henri had always been afraid that he would get in the way of the gospel instead of being a way to the gospel. He had many ambivalent feelings about his popularity because people tended to be transfixed by *him* rather than the God to whom he was pointing. At the same time, he needed to be at the center of things, too. John Mogabgab reflected: "I think he saw himself as a broken person who needed God's love and needed it also incarnated in the love of people with their hands and hearts who could touch him, hold him, and be with him when he was feeling sad. I think he really wanted people to relate to him, not on the basis of his achievements, but on the basis of Henri."

However, Rodleigh Stevens, a trapeze star who got to know Henri in the last years of his life when he traveled in Germany with The Flying Rodleighs, never saw that side of him and, in any case, clowns aren't necessarily wounded people, he pointed out. They might give the impression they are downhearted people and sad in their private lives, but that is only because people don't get to see their real faces under the make-up. Clowns can, in fact, be jovial people, and anyone auditioning to be a clown must display not depression but a good sense of humor and the enthusiasm to make people laugh. Clowns are easily stereotyped but come in different guises: some belittle themselves to achieve the desired result from the crowd, others are less demonstrative but still funny, while the mime clowns create laughter from their actions and facial expressions alone. "As we experienced him, Henri didn't fit any of these descriptions, though some of the expressions on his face did sometimes resemble that of a mime clown," Rodleigh Stevens told me at a circus near Frankfurt. "I saw from the lines of his face that he had spent many hours frowning or very deep in thought. He didn't show us any depression at all, but we weren't looking for it. We always remember Henri being very relaxed with us. He was like a child absorbing the circus life like a dry sponge soaks up water.

"Nonetheless, like a clown, Henri could laugh at himself. He knew that when he was making tea, he would end up boiling all the water away. But he would laugh about it. When he couldn't drive his little mobile camper home and I had to take over for him and park it, he was very aware of his physical limits. Again, he had the grace to be able to laugh about it. He didn't get angry with himself. When Henri imagined himself being a circus artist, it was done in a very spiritual way. Spiritually, he could throw himself into our act—he told us many times that, when he watched our act, he cried because it affected him so much. He knew how we felt. He knew we were aspiring to do something as perfectly as possible."

The Flying Rodleighs were struck by the priest's childlike qualities. He would giggle about anything he wanted to and found the strangest things funny. He commented on matters they thought trivial. He would chuckle to himself if the rhino didn't come in on time or how they reacted if there was an aerial miss. He floated on the cloud of his imagination. When he enthusiastically told them that their communication with an audience was "a picture in the air," they realized they were being artists with their act under a tent made of canvas. They were painting moving images with their bodies in various positions and poses. When Henri was entranced by their body performances, "it was like electricity going off inside him," I learned.

Henri met up with The Flying Rodleighs as often as he could between 1991 and 1996. From their first meeting, Rodleigh realized that the former professor of theology had a thirst for the circus life, which he was prepared to quench for him. Henri told Rodleigh that, out of all the circus acts he had seen in his lifetime, the flying trapeze was the best, not only because it was the most elegant and exciting, but also because it was the closest to flight. That was what he wanted—the actual feeling of defying gravity, perhaps. When the Rodleighs performed a specific trick of the Russian swing, in which there was a longer period of flight, he looked utterly amazed. "This is really what excited him because we had experienced those things that he had only dreamt about," said Rodleigh. "He was trying to borrow from us those experiences and those feelings because he knew he could never physically do it himself. By being close to us and intermingling with us as our dear friend, he was sharing our lives rather than being told about it. The celebration you have in circus is usually after the risk has been completed successfully. Henri saw this. He was always very excited when we were going to perform because of the risk element, and he would celebrate as much as we did when we had done a successful act. But if one or more of the tricks had been missed, he would be very concerned as to the reason why it had happened. No technical detail was too small for him. He asked a lot of questions about our lives, and we began to realize that he was not just a circus fan admiring an act but someone looking at our lifetime of discipline and dedication for ten minutes of work in a performance. You could see him feeling very sorry and maybe even sharing our depression if it had not worked perfectly every time."

Although Henri's interviews with the troupe were destined for a new style of book—perhaps even a novel—about the flying trapeze, it was never written. However, he published articles and made a delightful film for Dutch Television, *Angels over the Net*.[5] As a theologian, Henri was at his most original when describing circus life and the aerial acrobatics. University life had been about the mind, L'Arche focused on the primacy of the heart but The Flying Rodleighs gave him new insights into the body. A clumsy and unpractical person, he had never really been in touch with his body, but all that changed. He became almost fanatical in discovering over several visits what was involved in a flying trapeze act—the danger, the interpersonal relationships, the complexities of the rigging, the setting up, costumes, sound, and music. The performance was the result of immense thought, huge commitment, enthusiasm, and work.

However, a theological breakthrough came for Henri the day Rodleigh told him, "Everybody always thinks the hero of the trapeze is the flyer. I am a flyer. I do all these things—saltos, triples, and spectacular things. People applaud, and I think I am great. But the real hero is the catcher. I can only fly freely when I know there is a catcher to catch me. When I come back from my 'trip,' I know there is somebody to grab me." This led Henri to reflect on the fact that people liked to take risks and be free in life, but they also wanted to know there was a catcher—that, when they come down from it all, they're going to be caught, they're going to be safe. This had been a constant preoccupation for Henri when thinking about his own life and the life beyond. The great hero was the least visible and the flyers had always to "trust the catcher," a metaphor that he also used when teaching about dying. When he watched The Flying Rodleighs, Henri saw people who had to focus on their act and not think about anything else while they were on the trapeze, performers who did something with their bodies and who created community, first among themselves as a small group and then among an audience of men and women— young, old, all with their diverse backgrounds and languages. He saw that the troupe created a sense of family wherever they went, inviting people through their bodies, beauty, dance-in-the-air, catching, and flying to create community among community— something the world badly needed. "Who doesn't desire friendship, belonging, to laugh, to be free?" Henri asked. "Who doesn't need discipline, a sense of togetherness? It's all there in one act. It's what life is all about. It's what the world is all about." The act revealed more about theology than many books he had read. Although they would not say it themselves, The Rodleighs became theology teachers for the great pastoral theologian.

"The trapeze act becomes a symbol for the concentrated, meditative life," Henri remarks in the film:

The spiritual life is to be in the middle of a very violent, dark, complicated world and to be able to be there for a moment totally with God, totally present. Always believe that. Praying is to be with God and, for a second, to be able to let go of other things and to trust that you are safe there. Life is difficult. But finally, you are safe, and you can do something together that is beautiful. So, in a way, some of my deepest spiritual questions became visible in what they were living and doing. People talk about this as the last phase of my life, but I keep thinking of it as the first real one. It's always the sense that the real thing is always ahead of you. As long as you can fully believe in what you're doing at the moment you can trust it, live in it, and enjoy it. Somehow, the ability to be totally present in the present creates a glimpse of eternity, a glimpse of the true life, a glimpse of some of the deepest human aspirations, a glimpse of love, a glimpse of the kingdom, or a glimpse of beauty. You will soon know what real beauty is, what harmony is, what real joy is.

You are unlikely to find film or photographs of Henri Nouwen looking happier than when, like a child at the circus, he was watching the flying trapeze artists. Just as he walked inside a work of art to understand it more, so he studied the aerial acrobatics with commitment and intensity. On two occasions—in June 1993 and July 1996—he experienced what it was like to fly. After climbing the steel ladder, he was put in a safety belt with belt ropes going through a system of pulley blocks, controlled by a team member on the ground. "He said it was the most exciting thing he had done, he had never done anything as thrilling," said Rodleigh, noticing that, on the second occasion, their friend was in worse shape than he had been three years before.

> I was always concerned that the strain he had to go through physically would somehow affect him. I was really worried he would get hurt, or have sore muscles and a sore stomach but he never mentioned it to me. I did see him huffing and puffing. I told him to take a rest and not do more than he had to. But he said he would like the feeling of hanging underneath the catcher, the feeling of being gripped and being held by somebody, and imagining what it would have been like had he been a flyer and then been caught by that catcher. When he watched himself on video trying out the trapeze, looking very lanky, gawky and totally unprofessional compared with us, he laughed at himself saying, "Just look at me!" He knew that he was never going to be a great trapeze artist but that didn't stop his imagination.

There was a certain utopia about circus life that Henri responded to. Even when the artists were physically tired, mentally drained, injured, or grieving, they still had to entertain an audience. This impressed Henri. Whatever hardship they were facing, they managed to come out and be present to the audience. Likewise for the priest-performer, no matter how lonely or fragmented he was feeling, his wounds still managed to "perform" and heal others. "After Henri met us, the circus meant more to him because he could identify with it," Rodleigh Stevens said.

> He had a deeper involvement with circus life having traveled with it. At every other circus he visited afterward, he found a different meaning within it. But he always came back to us because this was where something had

touched him. Something happened to him with us that didn't happen to him anywhere else. He enjoyed every minute, and we thought he was always like this. We took Henri at face value and we accepted the person that he presented to us. We loved Henri dearly. We hugged him every time he came and before he left. We made him feel loved, wanted, and needed. It was genuine. It wasn't an act on our part.

In the final year of Henri's life, his interest in flight led him to ruminate on space travel. He twice watched the film *Apollo 13*. Looking at photographs of the Earth from outer space and reading the reflections of astronauts and cosmonauts, he comments in *Sabbatical Journey*, "I had a sense of being introduced to a new mysticism."[6] The observations reveal to him the precariousness of life, the unity of the human family, the power of love, and the mystery of God. He notes that the crew had been overwhelmed by the beauty of Earth: "Seeing your home planet as a precious little gem that needs care and protection is a deeply mystical experience that can only be captured by words such as *grace* and *responsibility*."[7] Studying an account by an *Apollo 9* crewman, who experienced his astronautical vision as a grace and a gift for all humanity, Henri regards him as a mystic or seer—Isaiah, Joan of Arc, or John of the Cross could have written in such a way. The human heart is united with the heart of the universe, and this unity becomes the source of a new mission. For Henri, the "seers" are like holy men who carry a special radiance because of what they have seen. Moreover, a recollection from a man on *Columbia 7* encapsulates the loneliness of the mystic: "Having seen and experienced what cannot be expressed in words must still be communicated." This reminds Henri of his own experience of priesthood. The sacrament of holy orders is a grace that allows him to see a vision. His call is to let others know what he has seen. For him, it is a long loneliness and an inexpressible joy. Mystical experience is divine grace that is always available to those who really desire it, according to the writer Andrew Harvey. Throughout their lives, human beings are given glimpses into the heart *of the real*, which they are free to pursue or forget. During his final year, Henri met Andrew Harvey, a poet, writer, teacher, mystic, and celebrated authority on mysticism across the faith traditions, after he had given a lecture in Oakland, California. Although Harvey's personal and intellectual history was completely different from his, Henri had "the deep sense of meeting a soul-friend." That evening Henri and two friends "discussed at some length the way Andrew's mysticism had touched us."[8]

FRATERNAL FAREWELL

Although Henri always hoped to live a long life like his father, he knew the importance of preparing for an event that might one day come upon him unexpectedly. Friends noticed how breathless he became when walking, and it is clear from correspondence that he was conscious of not being as fit as he once had been. In a card to Jan van den Bosch in 1994, he wrote rather pointedly, "I am extremely busy traveling around the U.S. and Canada to give retreats and workshops and to make the mission of L'Arche known. It is quite tiring, and a little bit too much of a strain on my physical health, but so far so good."

The following July, he visited an old friend, Joseph Cardinal Bernardin, archbishop of Chicago, who had been stricken with cancer. He took him a copy of his recent book, *Our Greatest Gift: A Meditation on Dying and Caring*. Exhausted from radiation treatments, Cardinal Bernardin listened as intently as he could as Henri spoke of the importance of looking on death as a friend rather than an enemy. "It's very simple," he told him. "If you have fear and anxiety, and you talk to a friend, then those fears and anxieties are minimized and could even disappear. If you see them as an enemy, then you go into a state of denial and try to get as far away as possible from them....People of faith, who believe that death is the transition from this life to life eternal, should see it as a friend." Cardinal Bernardin found the conversation helpful and the visit "very significant" for him. There was no doubt that, in the dying archbishop's mind, the writer himself was prepared for death.[9]

Not only that—back in Holland, Jan van den Bosch found Henri totally preoccupied with the subject. Imbibing the sea air together on walks along beaches, he observed Henri's utter fascination with death:

> We had long talks about it and he would say "well, tell me about the friends you have lost. What do you remember about their deaths? I will die before you and I hope that you would sit next to my casket and talk to me, and be with me." I didn't want to talk about it, but he brought it up on several occasions. I thought at times he was teasing but he was serious. I didn't want to see him when he was dead because I wanted to have the remembrance of somebody alive. He was anticipating his own death, knowing that something better was waiting for him. I don't know if he considered his loneliness awful, but it was a struggle, and death for him was an escape.

During his last year, Henri was not in the best of health, yet he traveled incessantly and was constantly exhausted. A Benedictine monk in Europe smiled as he told me that, during this so-called sabbatical year, Henri had stayed at a Dutch monastery to rest, but ended up rushing around and trying to persuade the abbot to allow him to give monastic "conferences"—spiritual talks to the brothers.

Jurjen Beumer, the Dutch theologian and diaconal preacher,[10] also noticed how often Henri spoke of feeling tired. On one occasion, Henri complained of chest pains while walking with Jurjen in Haarlem, near Amsterdam. They returned immediately to Jurjen's home and summoned a doctor who could find nothing seriously wrong. Jurjen would sometimes collect Henri from Schiphol International Airport after he had flown in from Toronto; they would then drive to an abbey to pray or Henri would celebrate the Eucharist with him. (On one occasion, Henri left behind at Jurjen's home his envelope of unconsecrated hosts concealed in a batch of papers, so the Protestant minister decided to use them for his celebrations of holy communion, using only half a wafer each time so he could feel more closely connected with the Catholic priest.) Henri tended to sleep during the afternoon before having dinner together in a restaurant and talking together long into the evening. Jurjen was particularly struck by Henri's observation that no person could satiate another's human loneliness, and therefore, men and women should not cling to one other. "I do not agree with those who say Henri was pathological," Jurjen told me. "He had the depressive tendencies of the Christian mystics. His gift was exposing his depression to us by saying this was something we all feel, though maybe he felt it a little more, predisposed to it as a celibate priest. He was a man of ambivalences with this deep feeling of not belonging, but in social gatherings, with his vivid spirit, you wouldn't have believed he did not feel he was the beloved of God. He put the question of loneliness on a deeper level. He taught that solitude was the place where the eternal God wants to meet you. We tend to fill up the sanctuary, that inner place, with other people. We need the people and cling to them, but it is impossible for them to fill this emptiness.

"A spiritual person never arrives, as the mystics knew, and as Henri knew in his searching and seeking. I told him he had to write a book about the mystics. He accumulated knowledge about them and gave lectures about them. It all went into his heart. His writing was essentially mystical theology. Before psychology existed, the mystics were describing very deep processes in people. Centuries ago, they were dealing with psychological questions in their own spiritual context of their time. They wrote about loneliness, the desert, of being on the margins of the church, of ambivalent feelings towards the church that they all had. They were deep suffering people, but they turned their suffering into gratitude. As a figure in late twentieth-century Christian spirituality, Henri is more in the line of the mystics than any other tradition."

Henri always hoped people would understand more fully that the deepest form of mystical life would always lead them to the most creative act of life. The more profoundly they entered into communion with God, the more they would know where to find the neighbor who was waiting for them. Henri sometimes used the image of a wagon wheel to illustrate what he meant. Instead of running around the rim, trying to visit everybody, people should move to the hub. If they lived from there, they would be connected with all the spokes, in any case. In a television interview the year before he died, he said,

> When you enter into the heart of God, you enter into the heart of the world, and you are connected with people in a very intimate way. So, the mystical life, the life of communion with God, is in no way taking you away from people, in no way getting you out of the social action, in no way getting you away from active involvement in the world or evangelism. The opposite. It is important to trust more that, when you are living in communion with Christ, you really live it in the center and that from there on you will radiate some of the truth of Christ without always being aware of that.[11]

In September 1996, while traveling from Canada to Russia to make a film about his book *The Return of the Prodigal Son*, Henri took a day's stopover in Holland. Jaap de Wit, who collected him from Schiphol International Airport at 8:00 that morning, told me that, when he met Henri at the exit doors, he seemed to have no problem at all carrying his two cases and didn't seem tired. Jaap helped him into the car and drove all the way to Hotel Lapershoek in Ziekenhuis Hilversum. He remembered that they had spoken of the fragility of life, the war in Yugoslavia, how life could be going well one minute and broken off the next. "We were very close and I felt immediately that he understood what I was talking about," Jaap said. "We were on the same level. At the end I felt a warmth towards him and that we had become close friends."

Henri had arranged to check in early and went straight to his room to rest because he had a production meeting in the afternoon. General Manager Marcel Bosman recalled that Henri had looked rather grey and had said he was tired. He wanted to go to sleep. "He went to his large room on the first floor but at noon called the front desk to say he wasn't well. We went upstairs, brought him some water and saw immediately that he was not right. So, we called the emergency services, which were here in three or four minutes. His blood level was very low, so they decided to take him straight to hospital. The fire department was called so he could be taken out of the hotel horizontally. He talked about his pain over his heart. He was cold one minute, warm the next. We constantly talked to him so that he didn't become unconscious before the ambulance arrived. The police told us to do that. But we couldn't understand what he was saying. I do not think he was praying."

After Henri had been examined at the hospital, it was confirmed that he had suffered a heart attack. In his private room, he looked pale and gravely ill. His brother, Paul, visited soon afterward. "When I first saw him, I thought he wasn't going to make it," he said. "He had a lot of pain and could not speak. I thought he was going to die. I slept beside him that first night in a private room next to the intensive care unit. He said some words but not much. He just prayed with his Bible. We are sure he was prepared. He gave me the impression that, if it should happen, he was at peace with it." Then, to the surprise of the medical team, Henri seemed to recover and, true to form, managed to arrange for a telephone to be brought to him so he could make international calls. Then people started phoning him too. A psychologist talked him through what had happened to his heart and how he should live in the future. A new date was set for the filming, and Henri started to look forward to making the movie. Friends said that, despite his preoccupation with death and the health scares, he did not think he was dying.

When Paul visited Henri the following Friday evening, he found him in a room with another patient, away from intensive care. "He was telephoning and telephoning. When I asked why the hospital had allowed him to have a telephone, he replied: 'Of course—this is my life. I have to work.'" Henri explained to Paul how he had received instructions about the workings of the heart: "I know how the heart functions. I'm now a doctor myself. I have to stay in for another week. But I have survived." Although he didn't do any writing in hospital, the new medical information was probably being stored for a future book on the spirituality of the heart. As Paul left, Henri insisted on walking in his pajamas downstairs to the front door. He told his concerned brother that it was important exercise for the heart. Paul felt he would need to rest for the next three months. Nathan Ball flew from Canada and, after a conversation, he and Henri said Night Prayer together. This included a psalm that speaks of "in the shelter of the Most High," "the shade of the Almighty," and "under your wings I shall find refuge"—the very words that sang in Henri's heart when he looked at the tent and wing-like cloak of the father in Rembrandt's painting *The Return of the Prodigal Son* and sensed the motherly quality of God's love. Henri didn't think he would die, but knew he couldn't be certain, so, in the event, he asked Nathan to tell his friends how grateful he was. Early the following morning, Saturday, September 21, 1996, Paul Nouwen received a call from his office to say that his brother was "very ill." When he and his other brother, Laurent, reached the hospital at 7:15 a.m., Henri had already died. "He was just lying there," said Paul. "We were totally shocked—in another world. I sent a car for my father and he arrived at 11:00. This was the heaviest moment because my father bent over towards him, kissed him and said: 'Son, I have to be there. Not you. I'm 93.'"

Paul Nouwen believed God had taken Henri "when he was at the top of the hill." There could have been more success, but the essential message would not have changed: look within yourself, we are all equal and God loves you. "I think I am more open now," Paul told me back in 1997. "Although I have to rush in my business and travel all over the world, I've changed, especially in the sense that I'm happy to be alone in the silence and I appreciate listening to that inner voice. Five years ago, I couldn't do that. I was that rushing man myself, looking for my career and more profit for my company. I am still doing it but now I hear that voice. It's a pity that someone, especially your brother, has to die for that to happen. Now I feel his strength through my whole body and sometimes I have a tear that our relationship became stronger after his death."

EPILOGUE

There is something infinite in painting.

—Vincent van Gogh

A year after Henri Nouwen died, I signed up for a week's retreat to his memory at Ghost Ranch in Rio Arriba County, New Mexico. Looking out onto multilayered cliff walls, red hills, and mesas, this spectacular setting gave the artist Georgia O'Keeffe the freedom to paint what she saw and felt, not least Pedernal, the flat-topped mountain to the south. A sanctuary for contemporary painters, Ghost Ranch remains one of the most memorable experiences of my research trip, with the bonus of getting to know women and men from different parts of the United States who had long studied Henri's work.

A sense of community quickly emerged. We also visited the Monastery of Christ in the Desert in Santa Fe without realizing that Henri had been there only the year before. Every morning we prayed from Henri's *A Cry for Mercy*, our eyes, when not closed, focusing on a table with small candles, a blue-colored paten, and a glass chalice. There was a stole and cross from Latin America, with posters of Rembrandt and van Gogh. I always remember a retired potter from South Dakota telling me that when he read Henri's books, he felt Henri was "thinking like an artist." He had an ability in any given situation to find something that was "maybe mystical, unusual, or below the surface." His words spoke not only to people's aesthetic feelings, but also to the spirit and the graciousness of all human life. "Henri sees and responds to our human predicament in such a profound way," Dick said. "Art wouldn't exist without our expression of it. Henri's expression of words, and the way he put them together, was pure art."

The retreat was led by Henri's former student Chris Glaser, who said he believed the way of the artist mirrored the path of the mystic: it was something about seeing what had been seen before as if for the first time, and Henri had exemplified that vision. He pointed out that Henri had also been compared with some of the most well-known Christian mystics down the centuries, including Meister Eckhart, Francis of Assisi, Hildegard of Bingen, Julian of Norwich, and St. John of the Cross—men and women who might have appeared eccentric on the surface but whose profound spiritual insights were borne often of suffering, rejection, and loneliness. Henri was a unique—and, at the end of the day, unfathomable—spiritual influence in the world of the late twentieth century. Some might wonder if he is just too unclassifiable to be granted a place in the great mystical tradition of the Church, the spiritual equivalent perhaps of the Hollywood Walk of Fame.

Chris Glaser sees aspects of Henri's life reflected in Evelyn Underhill's five stages of a mystic—*awakening, purgation, illumination, dark night*, and *union*—and suggests it is probably more helpful to think of "five dimensions," which Henri arguably experienced both sequentially and cyclically. An early work, *The Wounded Healer*, could be interpreted as an "awakening," an awareness that God comes to us in our vulnerability. Most of Henri's books reawakened him to this truth, each one recounting, examining, and reflecting on a particular weakness, injury, or suffering through which he drew closer to God. Loneliness became a thread linking all his "wounds with a view." Henri was in a constant state of "purgation," purging himself of his busyness, restlessness, worldliness, and emotional needs. *Eros*, the passion to be one with another, was the combustible fuel that fed his relationships with people and with God. Henri's "illuminations" emerged through Eastern Orthodox icons and Vincent van Gogh's life and paintings, and they culminated in Rembrandt's *The Return of the Prodigal Son*. Henri's "dark night" was his anguish following the breakup of the close friendship at L'Arche, which spiraled him into depression and six months of therapy. The fifth dimension, "union," is more problematic, but Chris Glaser points us to the four stages of spiritual development of the twelfth-century mystic St. Bernard of Clairvaux's: love of self for one's own sake, love of God for one's own sake, love of God for God's sake alone because God is loveable, and love of self for God's sake. Henri's union with God can be discerned in the third and fourth stages, said Chris. "I believe Henri came to see God as loveable, especially as represented by Jesus, and that he came to love himself more because he recognized himself (and each of us) as 'the beloved.' He loved himself because God first loved him." Henri's book *Adam* might have been the closest he came in testifying to that "union" because in it he writes with extraordinary mystical insight of his relationship with Adam Arnett, the first person he was asked to care for at Daybreak. As Jesus was physically present to his disciples, so Adam was physically present to Henri. Jesus was Emmanuel, God with us. Adam became for Henri a sacred person, a holy man, an image of the living God. Such intimacy beckoned Henri to become more incarnational and embodied in his spirituality, weaving the physical and the spiritual being, his outer and inner lives.

> This is a characteristic of the mystic and, like the unfinished book, Henri was a sort of unfinished mystic. It was appropriate that he left unfinished a project on the trapeze artists, The Flying Rodleighs, who came to represent complete union with God. They had taught him the *vital* (*life-giving*) importance of "trusting the

catcher," in life and in death. That he never completed this book is emblematic of Henri's own inability to let go. Instead of trusting, he was always trying to "catch the catcher" (take hold of God). This was anathema to the trapeze artists who would have broken their colleagues' wrists if they had caught hold of them, instead of trusting that the hands would be there to catch them.

In his biography of the medieval mystic, St. Francis of Assisi, the Franciscan teacher Richard Rohr describes his subject as "at once very traditional and entirely new in the ways of holiness, and he is still such a standing paradox. He stood barefoot on the earth and yet touched the heavens. He was grounded in the Church and yet instinctively moved towards the cosmos."[1] Rohr could have been speaking of his friend, Henri Nouwen, who had a traditional worldview but had brought God alive through dazzlingly original approaches, like his theology of the flying trapeze. A paradox? Certainly! He was always hard to fathom and seemed to contradict himself at times. Barefoot? Well, he only had a few clothes and would take the shirt off his own back if somebody else needed it. In terms of touching the heavens, when they were with him, people spoke as if they were in the divine presence. Rooted in the Catholic Christian tradition, he most definitely was, but his work became global, attracting people of other denominations and other faiths across the planet. Rohr points out that Francis was unique and authentic, as Henri indisputably was. Rohr says it is precisely our woundedness that provides our interest in healing and the power to heal others. "As Henri Nouwen rightly said, the only authentic healers are always wounded healers. Most good therapists will tell you the same."[2] Rohr denounces the mystifying of mysticism and, like Henri, believes the path of the mystic is not an esoteric journey for a few but within everybody's reach. Mystics have plumbed the depths of both suffering and love, and have emerged with depths of compassion for the world, and they can recognize God in others as well as themselves. Henri certainly fits the bill. Rooted in God's first love, as all mystics should be, he battled constantly with acute loneliness triggered by forms of psychological pain that seemed to haunt him throughout his life. Yet, heroically, he remained faithful to his vocation and offered compassion to the world through the vulnerability and conviction of his preaching, public speaking, writing, and pastoral care.

Richard Rohr, who founded the Center for Action and Contemplation in Albuquerque, New Mexico, spoke to me about his personal friendship with Henri. He was always struck by Henri's ability to describe inner experience and then connect it "with a crystal-clear God-centeredness, yet it was also a God he was still searching for." He was never glib or pretended to have God in his pocket, so this had made him believable and helpful to others. "He spoke more specifically to the American psyche and, on my trips to Europe, I have not found him as well-known or as popular as he was in the States—in fact, he said himself that he was hardly known in his own Holland," Rohr told me.

> I think he had an ability to understand the relational, psychological language. Even though he didn't use psychological language up front, he still had the psycho-spiritual understanding and explanations of things that Americans so appreciate, and an ability to talk that language and talk to that mind without really using psychological jargon. Americans aren't much in touch with objective language. We like subjective language. I think he was very good at that, while at the same time being utterly grounded in this objective, pinpoint transcendent reference point.

Richard Rohr recalled how he and Henri would meet up on occasions, walking and talking, and how he still treasured some of the letters he received from Henri. He also sought his advice once when he felt like a jack-of-all-trades and master of none. He was teaching in so many areas and asked Henri how he should best use his time. "His advice to me was that he felt my *contemplative* teaching should be my main work—maybe just that—and then everything else would take care of itself. I didn't necessarily follow that advice, but I knew where it was coming from. I valued it as love and advice from a friend."

This recollection offers further evidence of how Henri was thinking in more mystical terms in the later years of his life. Rohr went on: "I was influenced by Henri Nouwen's friendship, by his simple, warm God-centeredness which I trusted in him. I think that, because he had shared some of his own inner struggle and inner heart with me, I knew that God-centeredness to be something I wanted, I sought, I needed, and kept returning to because I saw how valuable, how important, and how rich it was in the life of a friend."

Another biographer of Francis of Assisi, Donald Spoto, makes some conclusions about the saint that could well be said about Henri—his pioneering search for God in the world, his fidelity to the New Testament, the seriousness of his life, his eccentricity, his sufferings, and his paradoxes. Spoto points out that Evelyn Underhill believed that, with Francis, mysticism "comes into the open air" and "seeks to transform the stuff of daily life."[3] This was evident of Henri also. The true mark of holiness, says Spoto, is "the character of a life that gives to others, that extends beyond the narrow frontiers of itself, its own comfort and concerns—a life that furthers the humanizing process." Holiness is about living close to God, a habit of being reflected in loving service, a hunger for peace and justice, and an active longing for concord among nations, groups, and individuals.[4] There is certainly a resonance here too.

There can be no hesitation that Henri was an authentic spiritual leader, not only in terms of his writings, but also in the light of his faithfulness to God through all his emotional trials and dark episodes. In terms of his struggles, he might well be comparable to mystics like St. John of the Cross or St. Thérèse of Lisieux; he was inspirational to the end in the way he stayed in the thick of his difficulties and never fled. With the most generous of spirits, he had the outer conviction and inner authority to announce a message of love and healing to a broken world—and he did it despite his highly strung, tense, and nervous temperament, which he knew was all part of his own paradox. Many people suggested to me that Henri was a saint—all my research and intuition confirm that he was—but he side-stepped any form of spiritual adulation and was much more aware of his failings.

Former monk Robert Durback, who compiled the Nouwen anthology *Seeds of Hope*,[5] told me that after he had sent Henri the book's introduction for approval, Henri had called and said, "Bob, you make it sound like I'm a saint who's dead." Robert reflected for a moment, then retorted, "I'm going to have to make an important clarification: you're not dead yet." Henri insisted on eliminating another sentence, but because Robert Durback refused to tone down his text, Henri declined to write the foreword as planned. Henri felt he had been overexalted.

Although he had always appreciated admiration, Henri was not someone who felt comfortable with reverence, as we discovered earlier in this study. Robert Durback said that, based principally on the person he met in print, he found Henri to be a profoundly holy man whose mind was that of Christ—he saw the holiness in person, too. He acknowledged also Henri's weaknesses—the fact that he was more easily wounded than other people, leaving himself exposed to being hurt by the extent to which he made himself available and got involved in personal relationships. "He did react and that was the way his spiritual journey had to be worked out as he dealt with these weaknesses," Robert told me. "I wouldn't call it hero-worship, but I just saw in him a man who was a Christ figure if ever I met one. In my estimation, he was a very saintly man. He was very much configured to Christ. That would be my definition of a saint." To some, this assessment may appear hagiographic, but I must confess that, when I wrote my account of meeting Henri Nouwen for the first and only time, I found myself using similar language. It was not my usual response to an interviewee, even one I admired.

An enigmatic figure in the world of Christian spirituality, Henri Nouwen nonetheless broke the mold of spiritual writing by producing mystical books with a personal transparency few other writers of his ilk attempted or attained. Yet, as a person, he is still difficult to fathom—and perhaps rightly so. The eminent Soviet filmmaker Andrei Tarkovsky, whose work includes a feature on the Russian iconographer Andrei Rublev, believed humanity should remain a question, and that we should avoid thinking that everything in life is straightforward or explainable. The same is true of our spiritual heroes. However elusive Henri may have been as a person, more than two decades after his death, his timeless words are engaging with a new generation of readers across the globe. Henri made holiness not a state of religious consciousness reserved for an elite group, but an accessible way of life available to anyone at any time. In an uncertain age, when some churches have lost their sense of the sacred and many people feel alienated from religion altogether, Henri J. M. Nouwen is not only an indispensable spiritual guide for the era but also a worthy successor to the great mystics of Christian history.

APPENDIX

Letter from Henri Nouwen to the Author

August 31, 1993

Dear Michael,

What a joy it was to hear from you and to read your beautiful story about your vocation....I am so grateful to you for writing this to me and telling me of my little role in your journey. I still have very good memories of your visit and our conversation, and I very much enjoyed listening to the tape. I promise to pray for you and to hold you close to my heart as you continue your journey....

Your stories about your encounter with the Prodigal Son picture are really amazing. God has wonderful ways to get our attention!

You may be sure of my deep affection for you and my great hope that our paths will cross again.

Sincerely,

Henri

NOTES

PROLOGUE

1. Pierre Leroy, "The Man," in Pierre Teilhard de Chardin, *Letters from a Traveller* (London: Collins, 1962), 15.

2. Michael Ford, *Wounded Prophet: A Portrait of Henri J. M. Nouwen* (London: Darton, Longman and Todd, 1999).

3. William Johnston, *Mystical Theology: The Science of Love* (London: Fount Paperbacks, 1996), 3.

4. Evelyn Underhill, *Mystics of the Church* (Cambridge: James Clarke & Co. Ltd., 1975), 9.

5. Evelyn Underhill, *Mystics of the Church* (Cambridge: James Clark & Co., 1975), 9. The book was first published in 1925.

6. Underhill, *Mystics of the Church*, 9–10.

7. Underhill, *Mystics of the Church*, 10.

8. Richard Woods, ed., *Understanding Mysticism* (London: The Athlone Press, 1981), 400ff.

9. Ursula King, *Christian Mystics: Their Lives and Legacies throughout the Ages* (Mahwah, NJ: HiddenSpring/Paulist Press, 2001), 3.

10. Brother David Steindl-Rast, *The Way of Silence: Engaging the Sacred in Daily Life* (Cincinnati: Franciscan Media, 2016), 39.

11. Henri Nouwen, *In the Name of Jesus: Reflections on Christian Leadership* (London: Darton, Longman & Todd, 1989), 28.

12. Henri J. M. Nouwen, "Life is NOW," Interview, *Fellowship*, December 1984, 6.

1. INTIMACY AND DISTANCE

1. Henri J. M. Nouwen, "Touching Stone: The Sculpture of Steve Jenkinson," *Image: A Journal of the Arts and Religion* 4 (Fall 1993): 14.

2. Henri J. M. Nouwen, *Home Tonight: Further Reflections on the Parable of the Prodigal Son* (New York: Doubleday/Image, 2009), 69.

3. Henri J. M. Nouwen, *The Return of the Prodigal Son: A Story of Homecoming* (New York: Doubleday/Image, 1994).

4. Henri J. M. Nouwen, *Reaching Out: The Three Movements of the Spiritual Life* (London: Fount Paperbacks, 1980).

5. For a detailed analysis of the theory, see John Bowlby, *Attachment* (London: Pimlico, 1997).

6. Henri J. M. Nouwen, *The Road to Daybreak: A Spiritual Journey* (New York: Doubleday/Image, 1990), 48–49.

7. Henri J. M. Nouwen, *Can You Drink the Cup?* (South Bend, IN: Ave Maria Press, 1996), 14.

2. THE INTERIOR CASTLE

1. Henri J. M. Nouwen, *Intimacy: Essays in Pastoral Psychology* (New York: Harper & Row, 1969), 119.

2. Henri J. M. Nouwen, *The Wounded Healer: Ministry in Contemporary Society* (New York: Doubleday/Image, 1979), 16.

3. Raymond Tomkinson, *Life Shaping Spirituality: Treasures Old and New for Reflection and Growth* (Buxhall: Kevin Mayhew Ltd., 2014).

3. DEPTH AND BREADTH

1. Henri J. M. Nouwen, *The Genesee Diary: Report from a Trappist Monastery* (New York: Doubleday/Image, 1989), 177.

2. Jim Wallis, *Sojourners Online*, April 18, 1997.

3. Henri Nouwen, *¡Gracias!: A Latin American Journal* (Maryknoll, NY: Orbis Books, 1993), 21.

4. Nouwen, *¡Gracias!*, 71–72.

5. Nouwen, *¡Gracias!*, 71–72.

6. Nouwen, *¡Gracias!*, 173.

7. Henri J. M. Nouwen, *The Wounded Healer*, reprint ed. (London: Darton, Longman and Todd, 2000), 19.

8. Henri J. M. Nouwen and Richard Foster, "Deepening Our Conversation with God," *Leadership: A Practical Journal for Church Leaders* 18, no. 1 (Winter 1997, republished from 1982): 114.

4. THE TRUSTING HEART

1. Nouwen, *The Road to Daybreak*, 10.

2. Nouwen, *The Road to Daybreak*, 47.

3. Nouwen, *The Road to Daybreak*, 49.

4. Henri J. M. Nouwen in the preface to Gijs Okhuijsen and Cees van Opzeeland, *In Heaven There Are No Thunderstorms: Celebrating the Liturgy with Developmentally Disabled People* (Collegeville, MN: The Liturgical Press, 1992), 6.

5. Henri J. M. Nouwen, *Adam: God's Beloved* (London: Darton, Longman and Todd, 1997), 38.

6. Nouwen, *Adam*, 18.

7. Nouwen, *Adam*, 3.

8. Henry J. M. Nouwen, *In the Name of Jesus. Reflections on Christian Leadership* (New York: Crossroads, 1993), 29–30.

9. Henri J. M. Nouwen, *Our Greatest Gift: A Meditation on Dying and Caring* (New York: HarperCollins Publishers, 1994).

5. WOUND AND BLESSING

1. Henri J. M. Nouwen, "The Self-Availability of the Homosexual," initially published in *Is Gay Good?: Ethics, theology, and*

homosexuality, ed. W. Dwight Oberholtzer (Philadelphia: Westminster Press, 1971).

2. Nouwen, "The Self-Availability of the Homosexual."

3. E. Lawrence Gibson, *Get Off My Ship: Ensign Berg vs. the US Navy* (New York: Avon Books, 1978), appendix B, 338. Spelling and punctuation errors in the original letter have been corrected.

4. John Boswell, *Christianity, Social Tolerance, and Homosexuality: Gay People in Western Europe from the Beginning of the Christian Era to the Fourteenth Century* (Chicago: The University of Chicago Press, 1980).

5. John Boswell, in E. Lawrence Gibson, *Get Off My Ship*, appendix B, 337.

6. Quoted in the preface to Henri J. M. Nouwen, *Love, Henri: Letters on the Spiritual Life* (New York: Crown/Convergent Books, 2016), xv.

7. Henri J. M. Nouwen, "Befriending Death," presentation to the National Catholic AIDS Network, July 1995, 9.

6. *NOCHE OSCURA*

1. Henri J. M. Nouwen, *The Inner Voice of Love: A Journey through Anguish to Freedom* (New York: Doubleday, 1996), 36.

2. Nouwen, *The Road to Daybreak*, 225.

7. UNITY OF SOULS

1. Henri J. M. Nouwen, *Bread for the Journey* (San Francisco: HarperOne, 2006), 14.

2. Isaac of Nineveh, *The Ascetical Homilies of Saint Isaac the Syrian*, 2nd ed. (Brookline, MA: Holy Transfiguration Monastery, 2011), 35.

3. Henri J. M. Nouwen, *Sabbatical Journey: The Diary of his Final Year* (New York: Crossroad Publishing, 2000), 123.

4. Nouwen, *Sabbatical Journey*, 124.

5. Nouwen, *Sabbatical Journey*, 125.

6. Nouwen, *Sabbatical Journey*, 125.

7. Nouwen, *Sabbatical Journey*, 125.

9. THE HOLY MAN

1. Michael J. Christensen and Rebecca J. Laird, *Discernment: Reading the Signs of Daily Life, Henri Nouwen* (London: SPCK, 2013), 29.

2. Christensen and Laird, *Discernment*, 27.

3. Henry J. M. Nouwen, "Pilgrimage to the Christian East," *New Oxford Review*, April 1994, n4, http://www.newoxfordreview.org/article.jsp?did=0494-nouwen.

4. Drawn from Nouwen, "Pilgrimage to the Christian East."

5. Henri J. M. Nouwen, *The Way of the Heart: Desert Spirituality and Contemporary Ministry* (San Francisco: HarperSanFrancisco, 1991).

6. Igumen Chariton of Valamo, comp., *The Art of Prayer: An Orthodox Anthology* (London: Faber and Faber Limited, 1997).

7. Henri J. M. Nouwen, *Behold the Beauty of the Lord: Praying with Icons* (Notre Dame, IN: Ave Maria Press, 1989).

8. Nouwen, *Behold the Beauty of the Lord*, 14.

9. Henri J. M. Nouwen, *Letters to Marc about Jesus* (San Francisco: Harper One, 2009).

10. Henri J. M. Nouwen, *In the House of the Lord: The Journey from Fear to Love* (London: Darton, Longman & Todd, 1986), 75.

11. Henri J. M. Nouwen, *Life of the Beloved: Spiritual Living in a Secular World* (Sevenoaks, Kent: Hodder and Stoughton, 1993), 81–83.

10. REVELATIONS OF DIVINE LOVE

1. Henri J. M. Nouwen, *Beyond the Mirror* (London: Fount Paperbacks, 1990).

2. Nouwen, *Beyond the Mirror*, 29.

3. Nouwen, *Beyond the Mirror*, 32.

4. Nouwen, *Beyond the Mirror*, 33.

5. Henri Nouwen, *Angels over the Net*, directed by Bart Gavigan (Richmond Hill, Ontario: Daybreak Publications, 1995), videocassette (VHS), 30 min.

6. Nouwen, *Sabbatical Journey*, 22.

7. Nouwen, *Sabbatical Journey*, 22.

8. Nouwen, *Sabbatical Journey*, 149.

9. Cardinal Joseph Bernardin, *The Gift of Peace: Personal Reflections* (New York: Image Books, 1998), 127–28.

10. Jurjen Beumer wrote the first biography of Henri Nouwen, *Henri Nouwen: A Restless Seeking for God*, English trans. (New York: The Crossroad Publishing Company, 1997).

11. Interview with Rev. Brian Stiller in Vision TV's *Cross Currents*, featured in "A Tribute to Henri Nouwen: 1932–1996" (Richmond Hill, Ontario: Windborne Productions, 1995).

EPILOGUE

1. Richard Rohr, *Eager to Love: The Alternative Way of Francis of Assisi* (Cincinnati, OH: Franciscan Media, 2014), xvii.

2. Rohr, *Eager to Love*, 16.

3. Donald Spoto, *Reluctant Saint: The Life of Francis of Assisi* (New York: Penguin Compass, 2003), 211.

4. Spoto, *Reluctant Saint*, 213.

5. Robert Durback, ed., *Seeds of Hope*, 1st ed. (New York: Bantam Books, 1989). The second edition was updated and reissued as a Henri Nouwen Reader by Image Books, New York, in 1997.